W9-AEK-905

ELEPHANTS are WRINKLY

Integrated science activities for young children

by **Susan Conklin Thompson**, Ed.D

Photographs by **Thomas M. Smucker and Keith Thompson**

Illustrations by **William Conklin**, Jr.

Music by **Gretchen Young**

Good Year Books

An Imprint of Scott Foresman / Addison Wesley
A Division of Addison Wesley Longman

Good Year Books are available for most basic curriculum subjects plus many enrichment areas. For more *Good Year Books*, contact your local bookseller or educational dealer. For a complete catalog with information about other *Good Year Books*, please write:

Good Year Books

Scott Foresman

1900 East Lake Avenue

Glenview, IL 60025

Book design by *Pat Barbee*

Photos by *Thomas M. Smucker*

and Keith Thompson

(except where noted otherwise)

ISBN 0-673-36315-5

123456789 - MH - 02 01 00 99 98 97 96

Dedication

This book is dedicated to Keith for all his interest, enthusiasm, and support.

Acknowledgments

This book was an interesting and challenging project. I thank the people who gave their talents and time to help in various ways. Thanks to Keith Thompson, William Conklin, Beth Wilkinson, Tom Smucker, William Conklin, Jr., Gretchen Young, Kallie Young, Hannah Young, Matt Jorgensen, Chris Jorgensen, Bradley Conklin, Chelsie Hess, Jasmine Gillenwater, Eve Huff, Sierra McMillon, Stephen McMillon, Mark Anthony McMillon, and Kyle Kuhn. Thanks also to the editors who have made this book possible: Mario Campanaro for providing the opportunity to write this book, and Roberta Dempsey and Laura Strom, who are encouraging and a joy to work with. Also, thanks to Jenny Bevington who helps to share my ideas with others. I give special thanks to my children, Kayenta and Rosalie, who are wonderful at listening, trying out, and adding to ideas. I also thank all the children and teachers who have inspired me in so many ways over the years.

Letter to readers

 ***When viewed*** through the eyes of young children, elephants are wrinkly, camels are shaggy, koalas are fuzzy, porcupines are prickly, crocodiles are bumpy, flamingos are smooth, and anteaters have sticky tongues. Children love to experience the world through examining different textures and materials. Many of you will smile when you think about how children want to touch everything in sight. With guidance, you can involve children in numerous activities that help them discover new things about themselves and the world around them. This book, *Elephants Are Wrinkly*, contains a variety of activities that encourages children to discover, experiment, explore, and create. It is a "do touch" book.

The book is divided into eight chapters. The first seven chapters center around an animal, such as a camel or an elephant. Each chapter contains interesting information, stories, poems, and engaging

activities about that animal and its texture, such as activities dealing with an elephant's wrinkles. The last chapter has a different format and contains activities that involve children in exploring a variety of ideas and textures.

Open the book to any page and involve a child in an activity. You do not have to proceed from chapter to chapter, but may find the perfect activity to add to another experience in which you are involving children.

The activities are open-  ended and give children the chance to discover, reflect on what they are doing, and try new ideas of their own.

Discussion ideas and questions are included with many of the activities. As you work with the children, you will probably think of many more ideas to discuss and questions to ask as you help expand the children's thinking, link what they are learning to the world around them, and give them opportunities to share their experiences and good ideas. All books referred to in the activities are fully cited at the end of the book.

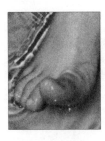 ***Encourage and praise*** the children's good ideas. Young children will astound you as they come up with amazingly inventive discoveries! I have tried all of the ideas in this book with children and adults, and have been delightfully impressed at their total engagement and creativity. After trying the ideas, I have added to many of them in response to the children's and adults' involvement and interest.

One of the things that always makes me smile with enjoyment is young children's total involvement in the process of creating or discovering. For example, when we were taking the photographs for this book, Hannah, a three-year-old who appears throughout, was involved in making a porcupine by poking toothpicks into a ball of play dough. She was so enthralled in poking the toothpicks into the soft dough that there was hardly a place in the dough left without a toothpick (although she did leave the tummy and face poke-free!). Afterward, she was collecting scraps of play dough from around the container and poking toothpicks into

them as well. It is extremely enjoyable to learn new things and to work with children as they learn. I hope you have fun with this book and that it provides some new opportunities for you and your children. I know that I certainly enjoyed writing it. As you try the activities and think of new ideas, please feel free to write and share them with me. I would love hearing from you, and in the meantime "do touch!"

Letters can be sent to
Susan Thompson in care of
Good Year Books
1900 East Lake Avenue
Glenview, IL 60025

Editor's note: Some activities involve eating or tasting. Teachers should ask parents about children's food allergies prior to conducting these activities.

From *Elephants Are Wrinkly*, published by Good Year Books. Copyright © 1997 Susan Conklin Thompson.

Table of contents

v

From *Elephants Are Wrinkly*, published by Good Year Books. Copyright © 1997 Susan Conklin Thompson.

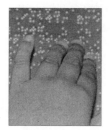

From *Elephants Are Wrinkly*, published by Good Year Books. Copyright © 1997 Susan Conklin Thompson.

From *Elephants Are Wrinkly*, published by Good Year Books. Copyright © 1997 Susan Conklin Thompson.

Chapter 1   Elephants are wrinkly

 Elephants are wrinkly

Wrinkled clothing

Dry cleaning & drama center

Wrinkles on faces

Fun in the sun

Land formations can be wrinkly

Elephants are wrinkly

Integrated areas covered:

Science, Social Studies, Math, Language Arts, Art, and Music

Activities

1. **Wrinkly hunt** What is wrinkly? Ahead of time, place some objects that are wrinkly around the room. These could include walnuts, wrinkled fabrics, leaf lettuce, and prunes. Ask the children to look around the room to find any objects that look wrinkly. Let the children, as a group, feel and describe the wrinkly objects. They will be interested in knowing that wrinkles can be grooves in smooth surfaces or creases in skin. What other things in the environment are wrinkly?

Show the children a model and/or picture of an elephant. Ask them to tell you what they know about elephants. You can record their comments on a chart. Talk with them about how an elephant's skin is tough and wrinkly. Their hides are anywhere from 1/2- to 1-inch thick, with a layer of skin on the top. This skin is very sensitive and even a small insect can really annoy an elephant! Baby elephants are born with soft brown hair covering their body. Adult elephants still have this hair, only it has become very stiff. They have not grown any more hair, even though their bodies have grown much bigger.

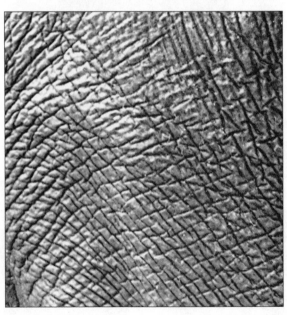

2. **Paper bag elephants** Children can each take a brown paper bag and crumple it into a small ball. Have them spread the paper flat, examining the wrinkles. The paper will be a good imitation of what an elephant's hide looks like. Let them examine the wrinkles with a magnifying glass. Each child can cut an elephant from his or her paper bag. These elephants can be displayed on the wall single file, in "herd fashion." Explain to the children that elephant herds consist of a family group that remains together for a lifetime. Small herds of ten to twenty elephants make up a family of brothers and sisters, aunts and uncles, parents and grandparents. Young orphan elephants may be adopted by the herd.

The children can also brainstorm which other animals look wrinkly and draw or cut them from a paper bag.

More information about elephants

- *An elephant cannot jump, but it can run quickly—up to eighteen miles an hour.*
- *Elephants have very long, full eyelashes.*

- *Elephants are excellent swimmers.*
- *Some elephants weigh 13 or 14 thousand pounds.*
- *Elephants are vegetarians and can eat from 300 to 500 pounds of food a day.*
- *Elephants are good friends to one another and help each other when they are in trouble.*
- *Elephants can live to be 60, 70, or even 100 years old!*
- *Elephants do forget.*
- *Elephants are bluish gray but roll around in the mud and dirt for camouflage and to keep off the insects. That is why they seem to be the color of the earth in the area they live.*

Resources on elephants

Elephants, by Joe Wormer

Elephant Crossing, by Toshi Yoshida

From *Elephants Are Wrinkly,* published by Good Year Books. Copyright © 1997 Susan Conklin Thompson.

Extensions

1. **Elephant food** Take the children on a hunt for elephant food. They can collect tree leaves, bark, twigs, and grasses. Elephants also eat fruits and nuts, so have some of these available to add to what is found. Ask children to estimate how much of this mixture would make a pound of elephant food. Involve the children in weighing a pound of food and putting it into a plastic sack. Children will be amazed as they think about elephants eating between 300 and 500 bags of this food mixture a day!

2. **Song and game** Children will enjoy holding their arms in front of themselves like elephant trunks and going on an elephant walk. Teach the children the song on page 5, having them sway back and forth as they walk. They can also try "hooking trunk and tail" by each holding onto a hand in front and a hand behind.

From *Elephants Are Wrinkly*, published by Good Year Books. Copyright © 1997 Susan Conklin Thompson.

Elephants are one of the easiest animals to train in a circus. Involve children in talking about tricks elephants can perform. Explain to them that many elephant trainers come from families that have been in the circus for many generations. Ask the children to imagine they are elephant trainers in a circus. Which amazing tricks would they like to teach an elephant? They may want to illustrate the tricks on a large piece of butcher paper, creating a group mural of many elephants performing.

3. **Read a story** Read this short story to children and then involve them in the activities that follow.

Louie the Elephant Trainer

This is Louie Delmoral. He trains elephants that perform in the circus. Millions of boys and girls have seen his elephants do their tricks.

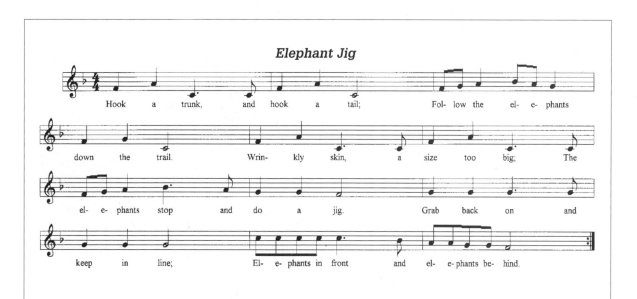

Elephant Jig

Hook a trunk, and hook a tail; Fol-low the el- e- phants
down the trail. Wrin- kly skin, a size too big; The
el- e- phants stop and do a jig. Grab back on and
keep in line; El- e- phants in front and el- e- phants be- hind.

These pictures (see page 7) show his four elephants. Their names are Jackie, Ronnie, Maude, and Misty. Maude was purchased from India in 1937, and the other three elephants came from different zoos.

Louie's father and grandfather also train animals for the circus. After Louie graduated from high school, he was taught how to be an elephant trainer by a famous animal trainer in the Ringling Brothers Circus. He really cares about his elephants. Louie says, "Every elephant has its own personality. Elephants are the most intelligent four-legged animal on Earth. I know all of my elephants well. Even at night, I am always listening to what they are doing and worrying about how they are. I treat them with respect and they respect me."

Louie likes being in the circus. He feels that he is lucky to do something he loves, and he has seen a million smiling faces. "It is worthwhile if one person is smiling and clapping. Then I know that I have brought enjoyment." The hard part is that sometimes he has a bad day but he still must perform because "the show must go on." One time he had a fractured ankle and he still had to be out there with his elephants. Another time, a tiger bit Louie's hand and almost pulled it off, and Louie still had to perform.

His elephants do many different tricks. They hold each other's tails with their trunks, jump up onto each other's backs, sit down, and turn in circles. All of these things elephants do in the wild. Louie teaches them commands to do these tricks. The hardest trick to teach an elephant is to lie down, because a wild elephant is very vulnerable to attacks by its enemies when lying down.

When the elephants are hot after their circus performance, they like to drink and spray themselves with water. They also like to throw dirt and hay onto their backs so they do not get sunburned and the bugs will not bother them. It's handy that they are wrinkly because the dirt gets caught in the wrinkles and offers them more protection. Louie feeds them lots of hay, and he says they love carrots. They each also drink about fifty gallons of water a day.

If Louie leaves the circus, he thinks he will probably work in a zoo. He can't imagine a life without elephants and says, "Elephants will be part of my life for the rest of my life."

From *Elephants Are Wrinkly*, published by Good Year Books. Copyright © 1997 Susan Conklin Thompson.

4. **Elephant myths** When someone says you have a memory like an elephant, what do you think they mean? There are two common myths about elephants. One myth is that an elephant never forgets. Another is that elephants are clumsy. Actually, elephants do forget some things. What things do you think an elephant might forget? Also, elephants can be very graceful. Discuss these common myths with children. Ask them what it means to be graceful. Have children reflect on the following: considering their size, elephants are graceful as they run and perform difficult tricks. So, when someone tells you not to walk like an elephant, you may wonder why. With the children, explore different ways people can be graceful. Some children have a wonderful understanding of what it means to be graceful. Consider this poem written by an elementary child:

Grace

She flies from the trapeze
Like an eagle taking flight,
Fireworks go off,
In the stillness of night.

So graceful and free.
If I could only be
As graceful as she,
All the things that would
be in store for me.

5. **The circus** Read Peter Speir's book *Circus* to the children, or read another book that contains illustrations of a circus. On a large piece of paper, let the children design their own circus, including acts they like. To get their imaginations going, encourage them to look at photographs or book illustrations of a circus and have them talk together about these circuses or ones they may have seen.

Wrinkled clothing

1. **Wrinkly clothes** Show the children an article of clothing that is very wrinkly. Ask them whether or not their clothing ever gets wrinkly. Involve them in discussing what seems to make their clothing wrinkly, such as throwing clothing in a heap on the floor. Discuss ways to prevent wrinkling by hanging up the clothing they wear or folding pieces of clothing neatly before putting them in a drawer. Demonstrate ways to hang different articles of clothing.

Have the children think about what they can do if a piece of clothing gets really wrinkly. They will probably have seen someone ironing clothing, but may be surprised to know that clothing can be washed and dried a second time and may be wrinkle-free. Also, sweaters can be washed by hand and then laid out to dry on a towel to eliminate wrinkles. Some people even take their clothing to the dry cleaners to have wrinkles removed. (See Clothing-care drama center, page 12.)

2. **Broomstick material** Ask the children whether or not they have ever heard of broomstick dresses or skirts. Have an article of broomstick clothing available for them to examine. Broomstick skirts can be

purchased in most clothing stores, or a sample piece of fabric may be obtained from many fabric stores. You can also make a piece of cloth or clothing wrinkly to resemble broomstick clothing by following the directions at right. Let them feel the fabric and look at the wrinkles. They will like shaking out the clothing and seeing how the wrinkles fall and stay in place.

Involve the children in thinking about and discussing why this fabric is called broomstick fabric. Explain that the material got its name because some people used to tie wet pieces of cloth into a knot around a broomstick to dry, and it was very wrinkly when they took it off. Even today, we tie broomstick skirts and dresses into knots to dry. The material today is also specially treated so that it stays wrinkly when it dries. You want the wrinkles to stay in because it is fashionable that way. Discuss with children what *fashionable* means.

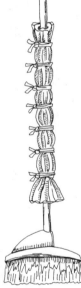

Then have the children also think about the invention of broomstick material. Explain that whereas an iron takes the wrinkles out, tying wet material around a broom handle puts the wrinkles into the fabric. Discuss why someone may have tied the fabric around a broom handle and how he or she even thought of this method. Involve the children in writing about their ideas and sharing them with a friend.

Have the children soak an article of clothing in water, wring it out, wrap it around a broomstick, and tie small pieces of string around it. When it is dry, the children can untie the fabric, smooth it out, and examine it.

An alternate activity is to have the children fold the material into a roll and pull the roll into a leg from a pair of pantyhose (with the foot cut off). It will look like an elephant's trunk! Hang the trunk up and, when it is dry, unfold the material. Ask the children to think of what else might work instead of a broomstick. Guide them in thinking of mops, pencils, yardsticks, chair legs, and other objects. They can feel these objects and think about whether or not the objects could be substituted for a broomstick. Help them recognize that a pencil would be too small, a yardstick is not round, and so on. Have the children measure the circumference of a broomstick and compare it to the mop handle and other sticks that may be handy.

How were different inventions discovered? Talk with the children about how we heat metal to take wrinkles out of clothes. You can bring in an antique iron that was originally heated in coals or on top of a stove, or have a picture of one for the children to see. Explain to them that when the iron becomes very hot, it removes the wrinkles. Today, we

add water to the iron to make steam for pressing. Ask children to think about how the first iron was invented. Try to iron the clothes with a cold iron and observe what happens. Next use a warm iron. The children can compare what happens with the iron at different temperatures.

3. **Tools** Encourage each child to bring a tool from home that he or she thinks is a good invention. Ahead of time, discuss how some tools are safe whereas others are potentially dangerous. Tell them not to bring dangerous tools such as saws or knives. It can be a can opener, a curling iron, a snap on a piece of clothing, a roll of tape, or anything he or she finds inter-

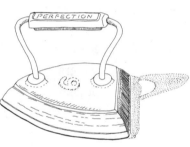

esting. Give each child a chance to talk about the invention. As a group, discuss what life would be like without the simple gadget and what we could use instead.

A fun book filled with information about small items such as tools, gadgets, and other inventions is Anno's book, *Flea Market*. Each page is fascinating and filled with illustrations of interesting items to discuss. Many of the items will be new to the children and will provide stimulating conversation about what they are, what they are for, and who could or did use them.

4. **Inventions** Some children may have invented something. The children can share their inventions and tell about why and how they invented them. Challenge the other children to invent something in which they are interested. Have the children brainstorm creative invention ideas as a group. For example, they can list as many different uses as they can think of for a coat hanger. For more structure, you may want to give them a box of old objects and have them use these materials, or you could create a challenge such as asking children to invent something that would make it easier to eat an ice cream cone without it melting and dripping on children's hands. The children can illustrate the invention on a piece of paper or try to create it using various materials. As a group, celebrate these new inventors and inventions! (See "Kallie Young, inventor" page 143.)

Dry cleaners & drama center

From *Elephants Are Wrinkly*, published by Good Year Books. Copyright © 1997 Susan Conklin Thompson

Activities

1. **Clothing care** The children will enjoy taking a field trip to a dry cleaners. Following the field trip, involve the children in recording the trip on a class chart. As the children watch, have them recall the trip and what they heard and saw, and record their words on a chart. Then involve the children in reading the story out loud, together. A good follow-up activity is to write the story on separate sheets of paper, have individual children illustrate the pages, and combine them into a class book. Each day a different child can have a chance to take the book home and share the field trip with his or her family.

2. **Clothing-care drama center** Create a clothing-care drama center. If the children have taken a field trip to a dry cleaners, involve them in discussing what would be interesting to place in the center. If they have not taken a field trip, you or someone from a dry cleaners can talk with the children and explain what happens to clothes at the cleaners. Also help the children think in a more general way about caring for their clothing. What do they do at home to care for their clothing? Do they wear an apron when they eat, and do they help wash the clothes that are soiled? As you are planning your drama center, include props that would be at a dry cleaners as well as some that are at children's homes. Also include as many props as you can that will give children experiences in reading and writing. For example, when clothing is checked in by the clerk, a child can mark boxes with words or pictures of shirts, dresses, and other pieces of clothing. There can be receipts to give back to the customers, charts about which clothing needs pressing, and even signs that tell when the shop is open or closed. Centers that include numerous opportunities for reading and writing are often called literacy centers.

Other sample ideas of props for a clothing-care drama center:

- *Baskets in which to sort clothing*
- *Racks on which to hang clothes*
- *Coat hangers*
- *Tubs in which to pretend to wash clothes*
- *Empty bottles of soap and starch*
- *Clothespins*
- *Ironing board and toy irons*
- *Toy sewing machine for mending clothing*
- *Cash register and play money*

Wrinkles on faces

From *Elephants Are Wrinkly*, published by Good Year Books. Copyright © 1997 Susan Conklin Thompson.

Activities

Smile

*A smile can cause a funny line
and give your face a new design.
And should you then begin to frown,
you'd turn the smiling line upside-down.*

Anonymous

1. **Wrinkly hands and feet** Encourage the children to look closely at their hands. What do the wrinkles or creases look like? Do they have many lines? Why are the lines there? Where do the lines go? What patterns, such as diamonds or squares, can they find in the lines? The children can also look at their hands through a magnifying glass. What do they observe? Is it different than what they were able to observe using just their eyes?

Ask the children to think about when they have been in the bathtub or the swimming pool for a long period of time. They will probably remember how wrinkly their hands and feet became from the water. Talk with them about how skin absorbs water from the tub or pool and expands in all directions and becomes wrinkly. The reverse happens when drying fruit. As the fruit loses mois-

ture, it shrinks. Because the fruit skin stays about the same size, even though it is covering an object that is gradually becoming smaller and smaller, the skin wrinkles up as the fruit dries. A balloon and tape (colored, two-inch wide packaging tape works well) can be used in a simulation which resembles this process. Blow up a balloon (this can be dangerous for children and should be done by an adult). Hold the balloon shut with your fingers so the air will not escape. Have a child wrap a piece of tape around the balloon. Then, slowly let the air out of the balloon. What happens to the tape? Why? Without removing or changing the tape, blow up the balloon again. What happens to the wrinkles in the tape as you inflate the balloon? Repeat the process. Relate this information to drying fruit, page 15. If you were to make ink footprints of a baby's wrinkly feet, they might look like this.

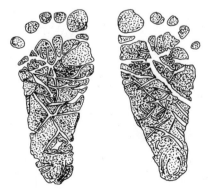

As people age, they also get wrinkles. Have the children bring pictures of themselves as babies and now. Ask them to compare what has happened to them as they have grown. Have they become taller? Has their hair changed color? They may also want to bring pictures of their pets at different ages—from when their pets were babies until they became adults. The children can tell you about the different needs their pets had when they were little from the needs the pets have as an adult. The children can also bring pictures of their grandparents. Talk with them about how their grandparents have grown older and the importance they play in a family.

With the children, look at pictures of older people. Have the children talk about the wrinkles on the faces of the people in the pictures. Explain that wrinkles represent experiences in life and the wrinkles really mean that these people have had a full life. You will want to make sure that the children understand that wrinkles are a natural, healthy part of growing older. Many children will know someone that has developed "happy" wrinkles because of how smiley that person is. These wrinkles make them look very kind.

2. **Wrinkles on faces** People of all ages have certain creases or wrinkles that give them character. Look at pictures of faces from a book or magazine such as *National Geographic*. The children can discuss different emotions that are shown through the creases. Explain that different creases can make people look pleasant, suspicious, mean, or unhappy.

3. **Faces and expressions** The children may look in a mirror and make different expressions. Ask them whether or not they can make their faces look unhappy, joyous, or show some other emotion. Have the children observe each other's expressions and discuss which creases contribute to how they look. Then give each child a lump of clay. Have them each model a face—nose, eyes, mouth, and ears. Using a pencil, let them experiment with drawing lines (wrinkles) to make different emotions. After an expression is made, the lines can be smoothed over with a fingertip and other ones can be tried.

From Elephants Are Wrinkly, *published by Good Year Books. Copyright © 1997 Susan Conklin Thompson.*

Fun in the sun

Activity

Drying fruit Ask the children what they think will happen if they place fruit in the sun for a few days or a week. Write down their predictions on a large chart and talk about each one with the children. Fruit can be dried on a windowsill or outdoors in the sun. Have the children wash the fruit. If some of the fruits have a pit, such as a peach, help them to remove the pit. The children can examine the pit and the place in the fruit where the pit was. Lay the fruit on a board or on a screen and cover it with a cheesecloth to keep it clean and free of insects.

If you are drying the fruit outdoors, bring it in at night. If there is not a place to dry the fruit outdoors, fruit will dry in a window with the window slightly open. The fruit should be dry in three days to a week. It will be wrinkly and leathery when it is dry. As the fruit is drying, the children may keep a daily log of what is happening to the fruit. The fruit will change color and become smaller, so the children can measure the fruit at the beginning and color a picture in their log to record the color— initially, again at one day, two days, and so on.

After the fruit has finished drying, discuss the process with the children. What happened to the fruit? Why? How long did it take for the different fruits to dry (do a bar graph)? Which fruit dried first and last? In what ways is the dried fruit like it started out, and how is it different?

You may want to have some dried fruit from the store available for the children to examine and compare with the pieces they have dried. How are they similar and different?

The children will enjoy tasting the newly dried fruit. The children can compare the taste of their dried fruit to that of fresh fruit.

Resource on drying fruit
The Little House Cookbook, by Barbara Walker

Land formations can be wrinkly

Activities

1. **Read a story** Read this short story to children and then involve the children in the activities that follow.

Wrinkly Land

Chelsie was excited and nervous. She was going to join her mom and her little brother Clay in California. Chelsie had been staying with her grandparents until her mother got settled in her new home. She had not seen her mom or Clay for six weeks.

Chelsie was going to fly in an airplane to California. She had never been in an airplane or taken a trip by herself. Her grandfather and his new wife, Beth, waited with her at the airport. Grandpa held her hand and smiled. "The flight attendant will take good care of you, Chelsie. When you get to California, be sure to call us right away so we know that you got there safely." Then it was time to get on. As she boarded the plane, Chelsie turned twice to wave good-bye to Grandpa and Beth.

A nice flight attendant smiled and took Chelsie's ticket. Then she showed Chelsie where to sit on the plane. A woman about the age of her mother sat next to her. She asked Chelsie what her name was and where she was flying. Then the flight attendant told all the passengers on the plane about their seat belts and how to put a funny looking cup over their mouths if they needed air. She also told them what to do if there was an emergency. Then Chelsie got a funny feeling in her stomach as the plane went down the runway and into the air, and she loved it!

Chelsie looked out the window and she could see far down below. There were trees that were only little specks on the ground. She was fascinated and stared out the window for a long time. Sometimes she could see houses and cars that looked like little models from where she sat.

The woman next to her leaned over and pointed out the window. "Look, Chelsie," she said. Chelsie looked down and saw brown ground below. "It looks wrinkly," replied Chelsie. The woman smiled. "That's because we are flying over rocks that were folded to make mountains."

The plane flew through some clouds that looked soft, bumpy, and wrinkly. The Grand Canyon looked like a big ditch with different colors of rocks in it. As Chelsie looked out the window, she saw some water, which the pilot said was Lake Mead. She also saw patches of land that reminded her of elephant skin.

"Everything looks so different when you can see it from up here," Chelsie told the woman. "That's right, it does give you a very different perspective or understanding than when you are on the ground," the woman answered.

As the plane landed, the wrinkly mountains looked again like the mountains she saw at home, and her mom and Clay were looking very happy and waving.

2. ***Aerial photos*** Aerial photos can be examined by the children, and you can ask them whether or not they can find a building, mountain, valley, river, or other feature (depending on the photo). This would be a good time to have a geologist or archaeologist come as a guest and discuss the photos and Earth with the children.

Information about aerial photos can be obtained and actual photos can be ordered from the U.S. Geological Survey at either of the following locations.

> *Earth Science Information Center*
> *U.S. Geological Survey*
> *507 National Center*
> *Reston, VA 22092*
> *Phone: (703) 860-6045*

> *User Services Section*
> *EROS Data Center*
> *U.S. Geological Survey*
> *Sioux Falls, SD 57198*
> *Phone: (605) 594-6511*

3. ***Creating a map*** The children can make a map from an "aerial" view using homemade play dough. Involve them in making play dough (recipe below) and then shaping it into mountains, valleys, and other formations. They can look at a picture of an area or location where they live and create the map to look like that area. Before the play dough dries, toothpicks or other sticks can be labeled with small paper flags and stuck into the dough, marking specific locations. After the dough has dried, the map can be painted with poster paints.

Homemade play dough recipe

2 1/2 cups flour

1/2 cup salt

1 tablespoon alum

3 tablespoons cooking oil

1 1/2 cups hot water

food coloring

In a large bowl, mix the dry ingredients. Add the oil, water, and a few drops of food coloring into the mixture. Mix thoroughly and knead. Store in an airtight container.

This is a photograph of a homemade map of Guatemala. Ask the children to find the person standing in the photo. Finding this reference point will give the children an idea of how large this map is!

Chapter 2   Porcupines are prickly

Porcupines are prickly

Integrated areas covered:

Science, Social Studies, Language Arts, Art, and Music

Activities

*1. **Prickly materials*** There are many things in nature that are prickly. On a table, place some prickly, natural items such as a pineapple, a twig from a pine tree, a rose with a stem, a cactus plant, pinecones, thistles, a small piece of a berry branch, or a leaf from a yucca plant. With the children, discuss each. The children will be able to hold and examine some, such as the pineapple, but others, like the cactus, they should only look at or touch very carefully. This is one time when the "do touch" philosophy should be followed with special care. As you discuss each item, encourage the children to share any experiences they have had. Tell the children that each item is prickly but also has a very good purpose in nature. For example, a rosebush blooms with beautiful flowers, a cactus is a succulent treat to many animals and some people, and pinecones hold seeds that can grow new trees or become food for squirrels, birds, and other small animals.

Read the book *Clementina's Cactus*, by Ezra Jack Keats, for a story that shows, to

Clementina's surprise, a simple cactus plant that blossoms with a lovely flower.

Show the children a photograph of a porcupine. Explain to them that porcupines are very prickly–an adult animal may have up to 30,000 quills! Have them carefully examine the porcupine and discuss what else they can see.

2. **Creating a porcupine** Give each child a ball of play dough about the size of a small potato and a small pile of toothpicks. The children can stick the toothpicks into the play dough, creating a model of a porcupine. This can also be done using a ball of clay and broken pieces of spaghetti or pine needles.

More information about porcupines

- *Porcupines live to be about ten years old.*

- *Under the quills, porcupines have a coat of thick, warm fur.*

- *Porcupines do not shoot their quills.*

- *When an animal bites or swats a porcupine, the attacker will get a mouthful or paw full of quills. The barbed ends of the quills stick in the attacker's mouth or paw, and when he backs away he pulls some quills out of the porcupine. This does not hurt the porcupine. A porcupine sheds quills as a dog or cat sheds hair.*

- *Porcupines are rodents similar to rats, gophers, and beavers.*

- *Porcupines have sharp teeth and eat bark and pine needles.*

- *Porcupines are also known to steal farmers' carrots, potatoes, and corn.*

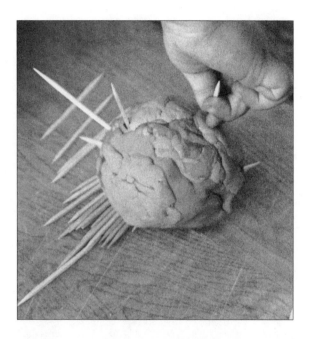

- *A baby porcupine is called a porcupette.*
- *Porcupines do not see well, but they have a wonderful sense of smell.*
- *Porcupines waddle because their legs are wide apart and short.*
- *Porcupines are good climbers and don't seem to be bothered by heights.*

Resources on porcupines

The Porcupine, by Carl Green and William Sanford

Wildlife of the World, by Marshall Cavendish

1. **Teeth impressions** Porcupines have very sharp teeth which they use to strip the bark from trees. You can find trees in the forest that have been almost entirely stripped of bark!

Children can bite into a small chunk of chocolate, making tooth impressions. Milk chocolate works well. The chocolate will need to be at room temperature. While the children watch, slowly bite into the chocolate and then examine the teeth impressions. Involve the children in slowly biting into their chocolate and ask them to examine their teeth impressions. What can they tell about their teeth from the impressions? Ask an orthodontist for some old impressions of children's teeth.

2. **Our teeth** Are the children's teeth sharp like those of a porcupine? Have several hand mirrors available for the children to look into. How many teeth do they have and where are they? What do their teeth look like? If any of the children have lost one or more teeth, how many spaces do they have that teeth will grow into? Tell the children that by the time they are adults, they

will have thirty-two teeth, sixteen on the top and sixteen on the bottom.

Children's teeth are strong and sharp enough to take a bite out of a crisp apple. They also can mush some foods and crunch others. Which foods do we eat that are crunchy? Which ones become mushy when we chew? Our teeth can also chew foods that are tough, such as steaks. This would be a good time to have a dental technician come to talk about how to take care of your teeth.

Cut a tooth shape out of white paper for each child. Involve the children in writing their own stories of how they lost or will lose a tooth. Encourage them to illustrate their stories and then have them share the stories with a friend.

3. **Porcupine quills and jewelry** As seen in the painting at right, American Indians used porcupine quills in jewelry and on clothing and accessories because of the decorative and hollow nature of the quills. Jewelry today can be made from porcupine quills. Quills can be purchased at many beading stores, but the holes are so tiny that it would be difficult for a young child to thread. Straws cut into sections can be strung on yarn and, although different from porcupine quills, resemble the hollow tubes.

National Museum of American Art, Washington, D.C. / Art Resource, NY

 *PORCUPINES*

4. Quills float Porcupine quills are filled with air. Explain to children that like a life jacket the quills help a porcupine float in the water. If you have a life jacket available, demonstrate with a child how to put on a life jacket. To help children understand how air in the quills helps a porcupine float, try the following activity with the children. Fill a tub or bucket with water. Drop a tablespoon into the water. What happens? Give each child a straw. Have the children blow through the straws while holding the end of the straw close to their hands. What do they feel? Next help the children clog up one end of their straws with clay. Now have them blow into the open end. What happens? Hold several straws in a bundle and wrap a piece of tape around the outside so it stays together. Explain to the children

that together you and they are going to put clay on both ends of the straws in the bundle. Let them help seal off the ends. Then ask them what they think will happen when you lay the bundle of straws in the water. Have a child lay the bundle of straws in the water. What happens? Take the straws out of the water and slip the spoon inside the bundle. Again, ask the children what they think will happen when you lay the straw-wrapped spoon in the water. Have another child lay the bundle in the water. Help them understand that the air is trapped in the straws and is holding up the spoon.

5. Song The children will enjoy learning and singing the following song "Don't Bother a Porcupine!"

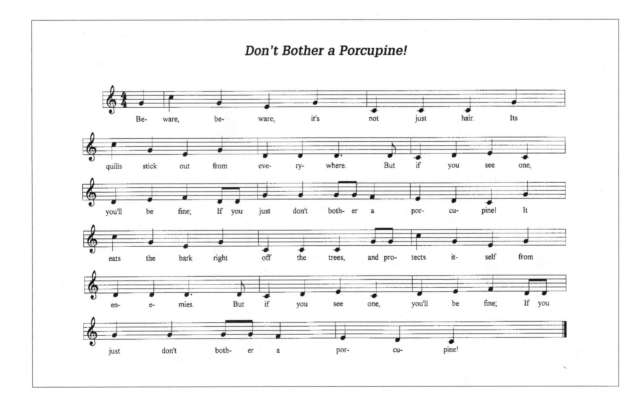

Don't Bother a Porcupine!

From *Elephants Are Wrinkly*, published by Good Year Books. Copyright © 1997 Susan Conklin Thompson.

Protection

Activity

Read a story Read this short story to children.

Tammy Batson: A Zookeeper

Tammy has always loved animals. She began helping a veterinarian when she was twelve years old. When she became older, she went to college and earned a degree in animal science. Then she went to school for two more years to become certified as an exotic animal trainer. Tammy really enjoys the zoo. When she was younger, she did not really understand the zoo and wondered why they didn't let the animals go. Now she sees the zoo a lot differently. In her job she educates the people that come to the zoo about the different animals. She says, "This gives them a chance to care." Tammy explains that once they know about the animals and what the animals need to live, they will understand more about how to help provide for them. Many people have misconceptions about different animals, and when they come through the children's zoo, Tammy helps teach them about the animals.

Tammy likes all the animals she works with. One of her very favorite animals is Priscilla,

the porcupine. Priscilla came from Medicine Bow, Wyoming, when she was a baby. At the time this picture was taken she was one year old and weighed twenty-five pounds. When Tammy brushes against Priscilla, a few quills stick in her uniform. Tammy explains that many people think porcupines shoot the quills, but they don't. She also says that porcupines are really shy, solitary animals. Porcupines, like Priscilla, have good memories; and if they do something once, they don't easily forget it. Priscilla's nose looks soft; but remember, don't touch a wild animal, even one as sweet and lovable as Priscilla.

What pokes you?

Activities

1. **Pet a porcupine** The children will be surprised to know that you can pet a baby porcupine with a zookeeper's help! If a porcupine is petted from the head down, the quills will lie flat.

Another prickly item is the bough of a fir tree. Let the children run their hands along a bough. Have them carefully run their hands the other direction and feel what happens. They may remember times when they thought something might be soft, like how the fir bough looks, only to find out that it was instead prickly. Some children will remember running barefoot in the grass, thinking it would be soft, only to discover that it is not soft but dry and prickly. Tell them that some animals are like that as well, and then read the following story.

2. **Read a story** Read this short story to children and then involve them in the activity that follows.

The New Kittens

Rosy and Kanie were wiggling around with excitement as they drove down the bumpy, dirt road to Lark's farm. It wasn't really a farm like the farm in the brightly colored book that Kanie got for her birthday. At that farm there were fields and tractors and a big, red barn. But the girls liked to think of Lark's as a farm because there were many white and brown goats, chickens pecking all around, a few horses, and ducks walking in and out of a small pond.

It was always exciting to go to Lark's house, but today it was extra exciting because it was the day after Kanie's fourth birthday. When Kanie had seen her friend Lark at

From *Elephants Are Wrinkly*, published by Good Year Books. Copyright © 1997 Susan Conklin Thompson.

preschool several weeks ago, Lark was brimming with enthusiasm about the new kittens her barn cat Tomantha had birthed. The mother cat was named Tom until she had the kittens and they found out she was not really a Tom but a Tomantha.

When Kanie got home on Tuesday, all she could talk about were the kittens. What a wonderful surprise when her mother wrote in her birthday card that she could actually have one! When they parked the car, Lark came running out with her mother. It didn't take long for the girls to run into the small shed where the cats were staying. On some old blankets in the corner of the shed lay Tomantha and six kittens. Actually, Tomantha lay on the blanket and the six little kittens were wandering around in the hay at the edge of the blanket.

"How old are the kittens?" asked Kanie and Rosy's mom.

"They will be seven weeks old on Saturday," replied Lark's mother.

The kittens were coal black with white on the tips of their tails and under their chins. It was surprising that the kittens looked so much alike!

"The kittens look just like their mom!" said Rosy.

Rosy was a year younger than Kanie and Lark. She felt a lot younger than the other two girls, even though a year is not much. It probably had something to do with how they always made sure she knew they were the older girls.

"Don't get too close to Tomantha," they directed her. However, they reached right out and petted Tomantha's head.

Lark leaned over and slipped her hand under the stomach of one of the kittens, lifted it into the air, and then handed it to Rosy.

What a soft little kitten, thought Rosy. She hadn't had many chances to reach out and touch the soft fur of a baby animal because she had only lived in a city. With a solemn look, she reached out for the soft little ball of fur. She started to take the kitten from Lark and then quickly thrust it back into Lark's hands.

"That kitty is too pokey!" exclaimed a surprised Rosy after feeling the kitten's tiny claws scrape her hand.

Lark's mother smiled. She told Rosy that the kitten had claws for protection, and that as it got older and knew the family, it would not be as "pokey."

The girls took the kitten home, taking turns holding it carefully in a towel on their laps. When they took it inside, it ran under the couch and pretty much stayed there for about two weeks, except for meals. Lark told Kanie at preschool that the kitten was a barn cat and needed to get used to the house.

The girls named the kitten Mr. Rogers after their favorite TV show. Mr. Rogers became a wonderful pet when he got used to the house. Actually, he preferred being in the house to going outside. Mr. Rogers loved to hunt and would chase the birds across the yard. Once he got in the garage and caught a mouse. The girls felt really sorry for the mouse, but their mother said that was natural for cats. When Mr. Rogers got older and they took him to the vet, the vet told them that Mr. Rogers was really a Miss Rogette, and later Miss Rogette had kittens of her own.

*3. **Staying safe*** Help the children to think about other animals that use their claws and quills for protection, such as puffers, bears, and hedgehogs. Explain to the children that this is nature's way of helping these animals protect themselves. Help them understand that they should never grab a squirrel or other small animal in the wild because it can bite and transmit diseases.

Ask the children to think about ways they protect themselves. Biting and scratching are ways animals defend themselves but are not appropriate for children. Involve children in brainstorming ways of protecting themselves, such as not riding with strangers, talking with adults about what is safe, not playing with fire, and stopping at curbs to look both ways before crossing.

In Barbara William's book *Never Hit a Porcupine*, Fletcher Fox goes out into the world after his mother gives him advice on how not to interact with others. The children will enjoy hearing his mother's advice.

Tools that are sharp

Activities

Whereas animals use their teeth and claws for sharp tools, people use many tools such as nails, drills, staplers, tacks, and screwdrivers. With the children, examine the different tools and talk with them about what they are for and how to use them safely. A simple book that introduces basic tools from the workshop is Ken Robbin's book *Tools*. The children can try using some tools, such as a hammer to drive tacks or nails into a block of wood. (Hint: Have the tacks and nails already started into the wood so a child will not be poked and will not hit his or her fingers while trying to start the nail or tack.) Also, the children can try screwing screws into predrilled screw holes.

1. **Tools and their uses** Other items children find around the house can be considered tools. On a table, lay a brush, comb, pincushion with needles and pins, fork, and other items that may be considered sharp. Have the children categorize them into groups according to their use. For example, some of the items may be used for cooking and others for sewing. Show the children how to safely move the sharper items, such as the needles, into the groups. Talk with the children about the use of each tool and how to handle it carefully—also discuss those that they will not want to use without help!

The American Indians used an awl made from bone for a needle. You may want to show the children a picture of, and discuss, an awl and other  stone or bone tools to give them a broader understanding of how tools have evolved through time.

2. **First aid for cuts** Even when we handle things carefully, sometimes we get a small cut or puncture. Demonstrate for the children how to clean a cut or puncture under warm water, dry it off, and carefully wrap it with an adhesive strip. Let them try washing an imaginary wound, drying it with a clean cloth, and wrapping it with an adhesive strip.

Emperor for a day

1. **Needles** Quills serve a valuable purpose, as do needles. The children can explore the useful nature of needles in the following activities. Quills are sharp and resemble needles. Both quills and needles are useful but can prick a finger! Read aloud the story *The Emperor's New Clothes* by Hans Christian Andersen. Although the weavers in the story are not really tailors, they do act the role. Talk with the children about how a tailor measures a person to see how wide and long to make dresses, shirts, pants, and other articles of clothing. The tailor also, at times, helps the person select materials for the garments and then cuts and sews the clothing together. Some tailors today alter pieces of clothing that have already been sewn.

2. **Tailor drama center** Set up a drama center where children can act out being a tailor and/or the emperor. Tools children can use include a tape measure, a full-length mirror, a wooden box to stand on while being measured, yarn needles, yarn, thread, blunt scissors, small tablets of paper to take orders and to give receipts, and play money for purchases. It also is fun to have a cape and crown to be worn by the emperor. (Be sure to tell children they are pretending to be the emperor but they should not remove their clothing!) Involve the children in cut-

ting newspapers or butcher paper into the fronts of shirts or pants as they measure and design. To help children learn a basic running sewing stitch, you can make a lacing card for them. First, glue a picture from a magazine onto a firm sheet of tag board. Next, punch holes around the edge of the tag board. Then the children can lace the card with yarn. Ahead of time, wrap a piece of masking tape around one end of the yarn to imitate a needle. The tape will make it easier for a child to poke the end through a hole.

Share with the children the lovely book *A New Coat for Anna*, by Harriet Ziefert, for a true-to-life story of a girl who gets a new coat after her mother gets the wool, dyes it with berries, takes it to a spinner and a weaver for cloth, and then to a tailor to measure and sew a coat. This and other similarly themed storybooks would make a nice addition to the center.

From *Elephants Are Wrinkly*, published by Good Year Books. Copyright © 1997 Susan Conklin Thompson.

Chapter 3

Crocodilians are bumpy

Crocodilians are bumpy

The mighty crocodile

Camouflaging for protection

Braille

We depend on one another

Crocodilians are bumpy

Integrated areas covered:

Science, Math, Art, Language Arts, and Social Studies

Activities

1. **Bumpy textures** What is bumpy? Help children explore bumpy textures by having them take a walk around the house, school, yard, or other environments. What can they discover that is bumpy? They may rub and feel the texture of tires, stone buildings, and a bumpy textured wall. Involve them in talking about the bumpy textures as they feel them. Ask them to think about where else they may have felt bumps. They may even remember a time when they were cold and had goosebumps! This would be a good time to do rubbings. Take a plain sheet of white paper and a crayon with the paper removed. Lay the paper over the bumpy object. Use the side of the crayon to go over the paper. This will "record" the bumps they find!

Explain that at one time many streets were made from stones or bricks that felt bumpy and were bumpy to travel over. Some streets around the world are still made with cobblestones.

2. **Crocodiles and alligators** Have a model or photograph of an alligator and a crocodile for the children to examine. What do they look like? How are they different? Point out that the crocodile is the only crocodilian that shows its bottom teeth when its mouth is closed. Ask whether or not children have seen either an alligator or a crocodile. Guide them in viewing the animal's back. How does it look? Does it look like anything they have ever touched (maybe on their walk around their environment)? Talk with them about how alligators and crocodiles are very bumpy. Crocodiles and alligators are in a "family" called crocodilians. Explain to children that a family name is like their last name. Use a child's first and last name as an example. Explain that everyone in his or her

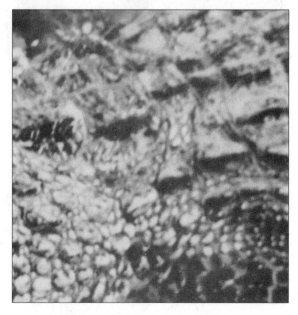

family may have the same last name, but each person is unique.

3. ***Creating an egg carton crocodilian***
Involve children in sculpting a crocodilian
out of egg cartons. Give each child a cardboard egg carton and have the children
carefully examine the bumps in the cartons.
Have them feel the sides, top, and bottom.
What do they feel? Using blunt scissors, the
children can cut the tops of the cartons
away from the bottoms. Have them turn the
bottoms upside down and lay them on a
table. For the top and bottom jaws, they
can cut the tops of the cartons in half,
lengthwise. Using masking tape, help them
tape the jaws to the bodies (bottom parts of
cartons). They can use extra carton pieces
to make a tail and teeth, which can also be
taped on.

4. ***"Alligator tears"*** Crocodiles and alligators are fascinating to children. Many have
seen the cartoon version in movies such as
Peter Pan and will be interested in learning
factual information about them. Actually,
crocodilians rarely eat people and try to stay
away from them. There is an old belief that
after a crocodile or alligator ate a person it
cried "alligator tears." We know that crocodilians do not cry tears after eating people,
but the children may still hear this expression when someone is pretending to be
sorry for an action, but really is not.

More information about crocodilians

- *A crocodilian's skin is covered with bumps.*
- *There are thirteen or fourteen kinds of crocodiles and two kinds of alligators.*
- *The crocodilian family also includes caimans and gavials.*
- *You can tell a gavial because it has the longest snout and most teeth.*
- *The biggest crocodilian is the saltwater crocodile, which can grow to be about twenty-five feet long.*
- *Crocodilians make nests and lay many eggs.*
- *Crocodilians can go underwater without getting any water in their noses, ears, or eyes because they have special muscles that close and keep the water out.*
- *Crocodilians eat mostly at night and have a fairly steady diet of fish, with an occasional bird, turtle, or whatever else may be within their reach.*

Resources on crocodilians

Alligators and Other Crocodilians, by Ruth Gross
Crocodiles, by Lynn Stone
The Alligator, by Susan Morrison

Extensions

1. **Learning about a compass** The crocodile always seems to be able to find water and will go straight toward it, almost as though the crocodile has a compass inside its body. Have compasses available for the children to examine. Talk with them about how a compass can tell us the direction we are facing. Ask the children to think of a situation when a compass would be very helpful. Tell them to choose a spot in the room or outdoors. Help them look at the compass and tell which direction they are facing. Then ask them to turn in a different direction. Now, what does the compass tell them? Have them read the direction from several different locations in the room.

2. **Body temperatures** Wherever people are, their body temperatures stay fairly constant. A normal temperature is considered to be about 98.6 degrees Fahrenheit (37 degrees Celsius). A crocodile is different because its body temperature changes depending on where the crocodile is. For example, its temperature goes up in a hot place but goes way down in cold water. Another name for this is *poikilothermic*. Lead the children in thinking and talking about warm places they have been. These may range from a hot kitchen to the sunny beach. How about cold places? Tell them that a crocodile has to live in places that are always warm. At night if the temperature drops, the crocodile slides into warm water. The children can use a thermometer to experiment with different temperatures, such as varying temperatures of water, snow, and sunny places. Have them record and contrast the different temperatures in a graph. Are the temperatures warmer or colder than our body temperature? How do the different temperatures feel to the touch?

3. **Body weight** There are few things cuter than a baby crocodile! Mother crocodiles help feed their babies and carry the babies around in their open jaws. A baby crocodile weighs about the same as a small bag of M&M's® and is almost a foot long, even though it is curled inside a small egg. To give children a sense of a small alligator's weight, have each child hold a candy bar or a small bag of candy. What else weighs about the same?

Have a child pick up another object in the other hand. Does the object feel heavier or lighter than the candy, or about the same? Have the children estimate the weight of several different objects against the weight of the candy. Use a balance to test the children's hypotheses.

From *Elephants Are Wrinkly*, published by Good Year Books. Copyright © 1997 Susan Conklin Thompson.

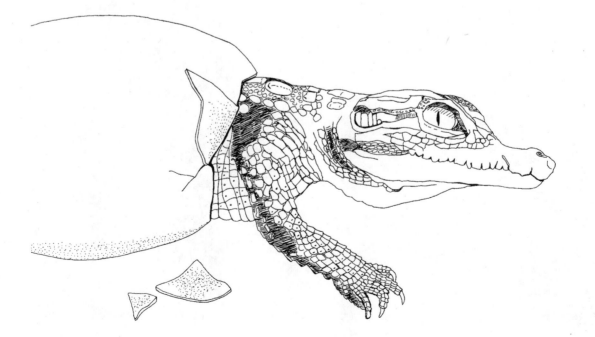

The mighty crocodile

Activity

Song and movement The children will enjoy learning the following song about the mighty crocodile. When they come to the line "My jaws open wide," they can position both of their arms straight in front and move them apart and together to simulate a crocodile's jaws.

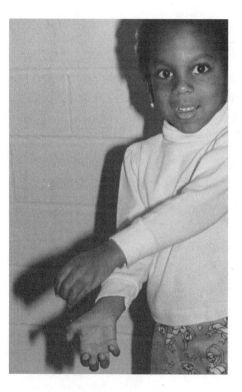

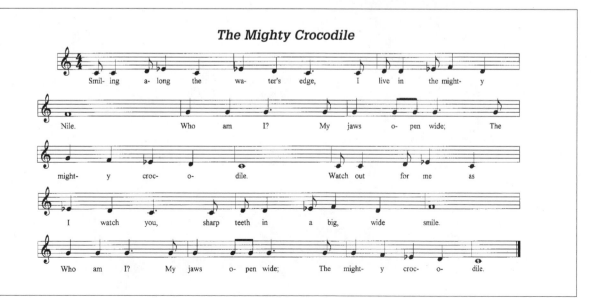

The Mighty Crocodile

Smil- ing a- long the wa- ter's edge, I live in the might- y

Nile. Who am I? My jaws o- pen wide; The

might- y croc- o- dile. Watch out for me as

I watch you, sharp teeth in a big, wide smile.

Who am I? My jaws o- pen wide; The might- y croc- o- dile.

Camouflaging for protection

*1. **Changing colors*** Have each child find an object in the room that is the same color as his or her clothing. Have the child hold the object next to his or her clothing. Ask the children to describe what happens. Talk with them about how a crocodile is a brownish green color and that it blends into its environment. We call this being camouflaged.

Many animals camouflage themselves by matching the colors of their environments. This is a good way for them to protect themselves. The lizard pictured below certainly blends into the rock on which it is poised. If you were to walk by this rock, you might not even notice the lizard was there.

This is an older iguana. The children may have younger iguanas at home as pets, as Kelly does in the story at the end of this activity section.

Show children about the large tortoises in the photograph below? Can they find one tortoise or more? Were the children fooled into thinking the tortoises in the foreground were rocks?

2. **A camouflage box** To further demonstrate camouflaging, give the children a box with one side cut away. Have them select an object and lay it in the box. Using markers, fabric, and/or crayons, they can color the sides of the box to look like the object. Ask the children whether or not someone looking into the box would think the object blended into the environment.

Children will enjoy hearing this fun story about Kelly and her pet iguana, found on pages 40–41.

3. **Read a story** Read this short story
to children.

Wanda

Kelly turned the page in her *National
Geographic* magazine, and there it sat looking up at her. The big black eyes seemed to
stare straight at her, and the creature almost
seemed to be smiling. Kelly could just sense
how well the picture had captured its personality. As she read the caption, she real-
ized that the lizard was a green iguana from
South America. Kelly made an attempt to
read the article on iguanas, but found it too
complicated, and finally gave up out
of frustration.

After studying the picture for a while, Kelly
had concocted a plan. She got up and ran
over to the big calendar posted on
the refrigerator.

"Mom!" she hollered. "Come show me what
day it is, please!"

Kelly's mom, Lianne, came into the kitchen
and pointed to September 1 on the calendar.

"This is today, September 1," she explained,
"And here is your birthday, September 7."

Kelly counted the spaces to the day that was
marked *Kelly's B-day*. "Let's see," she
thought, "that's seven days. I hope that's
enough time to make Mom see how much
we need a pet iguana."

The next day Kelly came home from school,
her book bag weighted down with books.
The books were hand-picked from the school
library. Four of the books featured stories or
information about iguanas, and the other
book was called *Ima-Jean and Her Pet
Crocodile*. Kelly figured she wouldn't have to
feel guilty about that book because, after all,
crocodiles were in the same family
as iguanas.

After hiding in her room for a while, looking
through her books, Kelly went downstairs
and approached her mother.

"Mom?" she said, a giggle rising in
her throat.

"Yes, Kelly?" Lianne said, without glancing
away from the tomato she was cutting.

"Well, I think I know what I really want for
my birthday."

Lianne looked amused. They had been having this same conversation every day for the
past two weeks. First she had wanted a
new bike, then a baby elephant. Lianne
could only guess what it would be today.

"What?" she asked.

"Well," Kelly paused for drama, "I want an iguana!"

Lianne couldn't help but laugh. "Hmmm, that certainly is creative," she said. "We'll see."

That night after dinner, Lianne found the subtle hint that Kelly had left on the desk. She looked through the books and just smiled. Maybe she could look into this.

It was the morning of Kelly's birthday. She looked at the pile of open gifts beside her, and at the brightly colored wrappings and tape surrounding her. She sighed, glancing at the unopened boxes. Only three presents to go, and still no sign of an iguana.

Kelly tore the paper off a small box. Her mother had purchased birthday paper with little green lizards all over it. Kelly had to give her at least a little credit for trying. She opened the box and pulled out a . . . hmmm, . . . it looked like a grocery sack. Puzzled, she looked inside. There were three little broccoli trees, and a bunch of bright orange carrots.

"What's this?" Kelly asked. Maybe this was some twisted trick her mom had thought up to get her to eat her vegetables.

"You'll see," was all Lianne replied. Kelly moved on to the last two presents, finding a long stick and a rock with a cord connected to it. "Hey, this is a heating rock! I saw one of these in my iguana book! Mom?" She looked up, but her mom was nowhere to be seen.

Lianne came into the room holding a paper sack. "What's that?" Kelly questioned.

"Well," said her mom, "it just happens to be a vegetarian, and it just happens to be the color of a lime, and her name just happens to be Wanda." Then, Lianne reached into the sack, and pulled out a small, bright green iguana.

"Wow!" Kelly said with the feeling of a small child who has just been given the world. "Wanda. I like that."

by Kayenta Thompson

Braille

1. **Read a story** Read the following short story about a girl who reads by feeling bumps–Braille. Then involve the children in the activities.

Nubia

Nubia moved to the United States from Bogotá, Colombia. Every day she rode the bus to school. Her mom walked her to where the bus stopped and guided her up the bus steps. She felt where the seat was and sat down. The bus driver, Andre, was always friendly and said hello. When the bus stopped at the school, Nubia's friend Juan helped her off the bus and into the building. Nubia liked to go to school. She had lots of friends in her room and they laughed and talked while they hung up their coats and put their lunch pails on the little shelf above the coat rack.

Nubia's favorite subject was reading. She loved to open the book and smell the fresh scent of the paper pages. Her fingers almost flew over the pages as she touched the letters. Her favorite books were ones by Beverly Cleary.

Nubia had not always been able to read so quickly. She could clearly remember slowly and painstakingly learning how each letter felt and how the letters went together to make words. When she was small, her mother had explained that she would learn to read Braille because she could not see and would need to use her fingers to read the stories. Nubia loved to feel her mother's kind face with her fingers. She had never seen her mother's face with her eyes but knew her mother's face well through touch.

Nubia laughed out loud when Ellen Tidbit's itchy underwear slipped down during dance class part way through the story. Then Nubia's teacher, Mrs. Kelly, told the class that it was time to put away the books. Nubia slipped it inside her desk, leaving the book open and hoping that later that morning she could read a little more and again enter Beverly Cleary's world.

From *Elephants Are Winkly*, published by Good Year Books. Copyright © 1997 Susan Conklin Thompson.

2. ***Using your sense of touch*** After discussing the story, talk with the children about how much they can tell about the world through touch. Place several objects in a bag. Take turns letting a child feel an object in the bag and guessing what the object is, solely through touch.

Explain to the children that Braille is raised dots. Have a book or card that has letters in Braille available for the children to feel. There are some children's books such as *Nate the Great* by Marjorie Weinman Sharmat that are written in words and in Braille on each page.

Using an embroidery needle, make dents in a piece of paper. Turn the paper over so there is a raised pattern to feel. Have the children feel the raised dots to give them a sense of what Braille may feel like. Ask them to think about places where they have seen raised patterns along with letters or numbers. Some children may have seen and felt Braille plaques in elevators or offices, or even along nature trails. Talk with the children about how important it is that we provide printed material that all people can read, whether it is through sight or by touch.

Some organizations for people with visual impairments have Braille bookmarks that can be given out to children, and some may loan equipment. If you can borrow a Braille typewriter, the children can type their names in Braille.

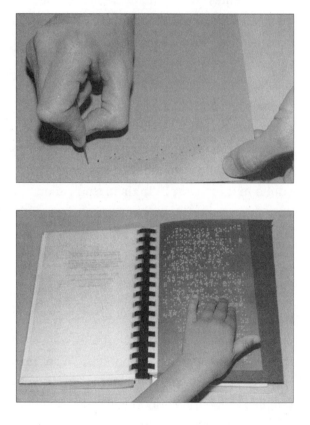

We depend on one another

From *Elephants Are Wrinkly*, published by Good Year Books. Copyright © 1997 Susan Conklin Thompson.

Activities

1. **Symbiosis** Many crocodiles live on the banks of the Nile River. With the crocodiles live birds that some people call crocodile-birds. These birds eat flies and worms from the crocodiles' skin. This is helpful to the crocodiles because it keeps them clean. In nature, when one animal helps another while helping themselves, we call this symbiosis. Talk with the children about how animals are dependent on one another for help. Ask children to think about who helps them and how they help them. They may talk about policemen, nurses, and special adults in their lives. Help them think about how they (the children) help other people. Have each child draw a picture of himself or herself helping someone else.

2. **People helping people** Which occupations are helping occupations?   Have a variety of hats and props for children to wear that indicate different occupations. What do these people do? Who else works in our building? in our neighborhood? in our community? Have the children discuss the occupations of special adults in their lives. Be particularly sensitive to children whose adult family members do not work for various reasons, and involve them in thinking of others they know and what they do.

  Talk with children about what they would like to be when they are older. Answers will definitely vary with the development of the child. A favorite answer is one from a three-year-old who had just been to Sea World and proudly told the group that she wanted to be a dolphin when she grew up!

3. **Emergencies** Talk about how children can help others in an emergency. On a large card, print the emergency number 911. Help children print it on a smaller card they can tape to the phone. Talk with them about what would be an emergency that they might report. Ask about emergencies in which they may have been involved. With play phones, have them practice dialing and reporting an emergency. Give them a low-key situation so they won't be frightened. For example, in real life a child may need to call and report that he or she smells smoke.

It can be very beneficial for an emergency worker to come in and talk about what to do in the case of an emergency such as a fire. Gear the presentation to the age and development of the children.

Chapter 4   Flamingos are smooth

Flamingos are smooth

One leg or two?

Flamingos are smooth, rhinos are rough

What else comes from an egg?

Waterproofing

Itchy or smooth?

Our hands

Flamingos are smooth

Integrated areas covered:

Science, Social Studies, Language Arts, Art, and Music

From *Elephants Are Wrinkly*, published by Good Year Books. Copyright © 1997 Susan Conklin Thompson.

Activities

1. **Smooth objects** What is smooth? Ahead of time, place things that are rough and smooth, such as shells, feathers, bricks, and sandpaper, on a table. Have the children feel the objects and put them into two separate piles—one group that is rough and one that is smooth.

2. **Flamingos** Show the children a model or illustration of a flamingo. Talk with them about how many flamingos have brilliant colors and are graceful. The feathers make the flamingo very smooth to touch. Have the children stroke a feather, and lead them in discussing how it feels. Ask them what else they can tell about a flamingo from looking at the model or picture. Many children will mention the flamingo's tall, thin legs. Flamingos are the tallest of the wading birds. How many of the children have been wading? Where and when? What did this feel like? When flamingos rest, they stand on one leg. Have the children stand on one leg. Ask them how this feels. Would they be able to sleep standing on one leg? Why or why not?

3. ***John Audubon's print:*** **American Flamingo** John Audubon's engraving *American Flamingo* shows a flamingo in detail. Show the print to the children and tell them that John Audubon was a famous artist who drew many different birds. As the children look at the print, have them describe the flamingo. Explain to them that different species of flamingos are different colors, which can range from white to pink-orange to coral. The word *flamingo* means "red goose" in Portuguese. Ask the children whether or not they have any ideas about why this large bird might be called a red goose. Show them a picture of a goose and have them compare and contrast the birds. Let the children point out the flamingos in the background. Tell them that flamingos live in large flocks or families. Sometimes there are a million birds that live together.

Scott, Foresman Print

4. ***Flamingo collage*** Have the children count how many people are in their group. Explain to them that they are going to create a colony of flamingos with the same number of members as there are children in their group. Lay a long sheet of butcher paper on a table or on the floor. Involve the children in creating a flamingo mural by letting each child paint or draw a flamingo, using a shade of pink or coral. Before the children begin, talk with them about filling the empty space so the flamingos will not be very small on the mural. Older children may want to create flamingos from construction or tissue paper to glue on the butcher paper. Backgrounds can be filled in with paint or crayon.

More information about flamingos

- *Flamingos make a loud honking noise like a goose.*
- *Flamingos often live in desolate areas along bodies of water.*
- *The flamingos' feathers keep them warm and dry.*
- *Flamingos run very fast, flapping their wings until they get into the air, and then they can move through the sky gracefully.*
- *Flamingos eat with a large, spoon-shaped bill, which scoops up and strains algae, bugs, and other food from the water.*
- *There are five species of flamingos. The most commonly seen in zoos is the Caribbean flamingo, one of two sub-species of the Greater Flamingo.*
- *Baby flamingos have grayish feathers until they are about seven months old.*

Resources on flamingos

A Flamingo Is Born, by Max Alfred Zoll
Flamingo, by Caroline Arnold

Extensions

1. **Families and colonies** Flamingos live in families and colonies. Talk with the children about what makes a family. Many children will have families made up of different combinations of people. Some will have extended families that live nearby, and some will have relatives that live far away. Others may have relatives both near and far. Ask each child to draw a picture of his or her family and any relatives that he or she would like to include. There is no "right" family; so if one child comments on someone's family, be sure to emphasize that families often look very different from one another.

Explain to children that a colony is a group of the same species living together. Ants also live in colonies.

2. **Shades of color** Flamingos range in color from white to dark coral. They are naturally white, but when they eat certain crustaceans that have red or yellow pigments in them, the flamingos turn different shades of pink. These colors are almost like a bright sunset on a clear night. Have children paint strokes up and down across a piece of paper as they experiment with moving from white to light pink, coral, dark pink, and dark coral. The color gradation can be made by starting with white and adding small amounts of red and yellow to the white.

3. **Flamingo bills** Flamingos have very unusual bills. They are large, curved, and pointed upside-down. The flamingo moves along in the water, filling the bill with sand,

strainer. They can use a sponge (which has been soaked in water so it will not absorb too much more water) to act as a tongue as they push the liquid through the strainer to see what remains. Involve them in closely examining the remaining particles. What stayed in the strainer? What did not? Are the things that stayed in the strainer different from those that did not? What differences are there (size, shape, and color)?

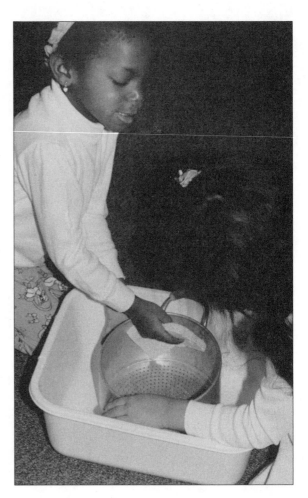

algae, water, and small bugs. Then with its large tongue, it pushes the water out through its bill, which works like a sieve as it filters out small creatures from the water and sand. To demonstrate this action, have the children scoop up gravel, sand, mud, and small bits of leaves, mix them with water, and pour the mixture into a fine

One leg or two?

Activities

1. **Song and movement** One of the most charming sights is to see a flamingo standing gracefully on one leg. Sing the song below with the children and then lead them in trying some balance activities of their own.

2. **On one leg** A flamingo is graceful as it stands on one leg. Ask the children to try standing on their right legs with their left legs folded up. How does this feel? Is it more difficult than standing on two legs? Is it easier to stay balanced on one leg if children stare at one spot on the ground in front

of them? Have them try standing on their left legs while folding their right legs up. Is

this more difficult, easier, or the same? Can they hop on one leg? How many hops can they do?

When the children fold one of their legs back, it is actually folded the opposite way from the flamingo's leg. A flamingo's leg folds forward when

Flamingos

Fla- min- gos stand- ing on the zoo lawn; All with smooth feath- ers the
col- or of dawn. Fla- min- gos stand- ing straight and tall;
Won- der- ful bal- ance pre- vents a fall. A more grace- ful sight you'll
nev- er see; One straight leg and one bend- ed knee.

the flamingo sits down, bending like an elbow. Have the children move the lower part of their arms and watch in which direction the arms move as they fold them up.

The flamingo stands on its toes. Have the children stand up as tall as they can on their toes. What happens? Have any of them seen ballerinas wearing toe shoes to help them stand on their toes? Explain that

flamingos have webbed feet that keep them from sinking into the mud as they wade.

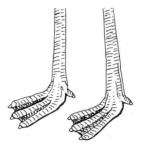

Are there other birds that stand as tall as the flamingo? Many children may be familiar with the stork but may be surprised to know that storks also have very tall legs.

3. **Flying gracefully** Flamingos fly very gracefully and, when viewed from above or below, each actually looks like a cross in the sky. Show the children the illustration below of flamingos flying, and talk with them about how amazing it is that such tall birds can fly so smoothly and gracefully. When we see a flamingo flying in the sky and compare it to a cross, we are comparing it to a shape with which we are familiar.

Ask the children to look around their environment to see whether or not they can find other shapes, such as a bush that looks like a triangle or a building that is square. A good picture book for looking at shapes in the environment is the book *Shapes, Shapes, Shapes* by Tana Hoban.

Flamingos are smooth, rhinos are rough

Activities

1. **Rough and smooth textures** Take a nature hike or a hike around the playground. Ask the children to look carefully around them to see and feel things that are rough or smooth. They may feel such things as plants, bricks, windows, and bark. Discuss the different textures with the children.

Have natural materials available for the children to examine and feel that are rough and smooth. Rocks, pinecones, and most tree branches will feel rough. Pussy willows, cattails, water stones, and most plant stems are smooth. The children can feel the materials and talk about the differences. Have them group materials according to rough and smooth, large and small, and growing and nongrowing.

Which animals are smooth like a dolphin and which animals are rough like a rhinoceros? The children can group pictures of animals, plastic zoo animals, or animal crackers according to these textures. Some animals may not fit into either of these categories (like the prickly porcupine) and can be in a category of their own.

2. **Sanding wood** Bring in wood that is smooth and other boards or blocks of wood that feel rough. Have different grits of sandpaper (fine, medium, coarse) available for the children to use as they practice sanding a piece of wood from rough to smooth. Sandpaper can be wrapped around a block of wood for easier use during sanding. Guide the children in talking about the process of sanding the wood and what happens as it goes from rough to smooth.

3. **Rough tongues and faces** Ask the children whether or not they have ever felt skin that is rough like the sandpaper. They may mention a man's face when he has not shaved in a while. Have they ever felt a cat's tongue? Explain that a cat's tongue is rough so that it can clean off the dirt from its fur. It also feels scratchy like fine-grained sandpaper. For fun, the children may want to draw a cat with its tongue sticking out and add sandpaper cut to the shape of the tongue. Or they could draw a man's face and add sandpaper to the chin and cheeks.

4. **Our skin** Have the children feel their own skin. Is the skin on their faces smoother than the skin on their arms? How about the skin on their legs? Give each child a small amount of lotion to rub into the skin on his or her arms or legs. How does their skin feel now? Have a bath bead available for them to examine. Explain to them that the beads are filled with oil and that when people drop them into the bathwater, the beads dissolve and the oil in the water makes their skin softer. Birds make oil naturally to keep the water out of their feathers and away from their bodies. (See Activity 5.)

5. **Feathers and hair** Have the children feel and run their hands down several feathers you have provided. Talk with them about how feathers keep a bird warm in the same way the children's hair protects their heads from the cold. How does the feather feel? Have the children run their hands down their hair and compare it to the feather. Explain to them that a bird takes care of its feathers by cleaning them and pulling out the loose ones. We call this preening. Sometimes when people are spending a lot of time grooming themselves and styling their hair we call this "preening" (after the bird's action). What do the children do to take care of their hair? Involve them in discussing how they keep it clean, how they must brush or comb it every day, and how they should never go to sleep with chewing gum in their mouths (gum could end up in their hair or they could choke). Children that swim a lot may want to discuss different shampoos they use to take the chlorine out of their hair, or how they protect it with a swim cap.

From *Elephants Are Wrinkly*, published by Good Year Books. Copyright © 1997 Susan Conklin Thompson.

What else comes from an egg?

Activities

1. **Flamingo nests** Flamingos build their nests in the water away from the land. They use their feet to press mud into a large (twenty to thirty inches in diameter), cone-shaped nest. Use a yardstick or tape measure and butcher paper to draw the size of the nest. Ask the children why birds make nests for their eggs. Tell the children that flamingos are good parents and turn the eggs every few hours. The baby has to work hard to break out of the egg— sometimes it works an entire day!

2. **Birds and eggs** What other animals come from an egg? There will be many birds with which the children are familiar, from chicks to goslings. As the children mention different kinds of birds, talk with them a little about each one. A book that helps children learn to identify several birds is Ashley Wolff's *A Year of Birds*. Point out that all birds come from eggs and have feathers. Contact your local Audubon Society for guest speakers and materials such as bird charts and guidebooks.

The children may be surprised to learn that a hummingbird lays the smallest egg. Its eggs are so small that ten can fit into a tea-

From *Elephants Are Wrinkly*, published by Good Year Books. Copyright © 1997 Susan Conklin Thompson.

spoon. Give each child a lump of clay and a plastic spoon. What size eggs must be made to fit ten into the spoon? Compare the hummingbird eggs they made to a chicken egg.

3. **Imprinting** When a gosling hatches out of an egg, it bonds with the first thing it sees, whether it is a goose or a person! This is called imprinting, and it follows this "Mom" around. For a fun game, have one child be the mother goose. Each of the other children can roll himself or herself into a ball shape and pretend that he or she is hatching. Then play follow the leader, imitating the actions of, and following, the mother wherever she goes. Have the children take turns being the goslings and the mother.

4. **Follow the leader** The children may have seen other animals following one another in a straight line. Cows will follow a lead cow in single file across a hill or down a trail, as will sheep. Talk with the children about the advantages and disadvantages to following a leader. The children will have experiences in which they have followed another child in doing something that was a good experience and other times when it was not a good idea. Children can make a print of cows or sheep following one another across a page by cutting the silhouette of a sheep or cow out of a polystyrene meat tray from a grocery store (a potato or sponge could be used instead). Have the children paint the bottom surface of the cow or sheep silhouette with paint and press it onto a sheet of paper to make a print. Repeat the process until the line of animals is completed.

5. **Birds and reptiles come from eggs** You can talk with the children about how birds are different from mammals. On a large chart, list what the children know to be different between mammals and birds, such as birds have bones that are hollow whereas mammals do not. Bring in cleaned chicken or turkey bones for the children to examine. Other differences include birds eat a lot more in proportion to their body weight than mammals do because they burn so much energy when they fly, and female mammals give birth to live animals whereas birds lay eggs. Then talk about things that are the same for birds and mammals, such as they both eat food and nurture their young. Note that reptiles and birds also come from eggs, but have little else in common.

Waterproofing

1. ***Waterproofed items*** Flamingos and other birds preen their feathers. As they preen, they spread their body oil, and this makes them waterproof. Have the children soak different materials in water—some that are waterproof and others that are not. The waterproof materials or items could include rubber boots, rain slickers, material from some types of umbrellas, and a piece of a tarp. The items that are not waterproof may be shoes, a sweater, a blanket, and a hat. As the children experiment soaking the materials in the water, encourage them to talk about what is happening and what they are discovering. What differences do they see among the items? Can they tell which ones are made with materials that are waterproof or have been waterproofed? Which pieces of clothing would they want to be wearing if it were raining? The children can use an eyedropper to place drops of water onto gathered bird feathers. What happens to the water?

Read Taro Yashima's book *Umbrella* to the children. It is a story about a girl, Momo, who gets rubber boots and an umbrella for her birthday. When the raindrops hit the umbrella, they make thumps that sound like music. Involve the children in sharing experiences they may have had in the rain with an umbrella.

We can waterproof tents, boots, and other articles. With the children, waterproof a boot using a waterproofing oil or wax.

Have stainless steel and rusty items (nothing with sharp edges) for the children to examine. Have children put on rubber or plastic gloves before handling rusty items. You may want to have them wear paint smocks. Ask them what they think happened to the rusty items. Some children will point out that they got wet, and the orange coloring is really rust. Explain to the children that the stainless steel items are made with a special metal so they will not rust when they are wet. Both metals are really waterproof, though.

2. **Removing oil from feathers** The oil a flamingo uses on its feathers is very different from the oil a flamingo or other bird would have on it if it were caught in an oil spill. The flamingo's own oil is a natural body oil, whereas the crude oil from a spill is not. Talk with the children about how dangerous an oil spill can be for wildlife. Have the children put on paint smocks, then distribute feathers that have been dipped in 10W30 motor oil. Give the children a small dish, string, paper towels, fabric scraps, water, and a liquid grease-fighting dish detergent such as Dawn®. Challenge them to see whether or not they can get the feathers clean using any or all of the above materials. Have them record their efforts and results in a notebook. What did they discover? Which method worked best to remove the oil? Do they think it would be difficult to clean crude oil from a large colony of flamingos? Why or why not? Help them call a forest ranger and talk with him or her (or arrange for one to come and talk) about what happens to animals in an oil spill and how people try to clean the oil off the animals' feathers, skin, and fur.

3. **Water and crayon resist** Give each child or group of children a piece of waxed paper. With an eyedropper or using a cotton

swab, have them drop drops of water onto the waxed paper. What happens to each drop? How about 50 drops? Now give them a piece of paper bag or paper towel. Have them try the drops again. Did the drops react differently on the waxed paper than on the paper bag or paper towel? Why? Help children think about how the surface of the waxed paper made the difference. The drops did not sink into the surface of the waxed paper because the wax resisted the water. If they needed to clean up a spilled liquid, would they want to use the waxed paper or the paper towel? When they were cleaning off the feathers, did they find that the oil also resisted the water? The resist principle can be further experimented with by having children use crayons to color a picture and then water-paint over the drawing. The crayon will resist the paint, but the part of the page without the crayon will absorb the paint.

Itchy or smooth?

Activities

1. **Itchy clothing** The flamingo's feathers feel smooth. The feathers are really the flamingo's clothing. Ask the children to feel their own clothing. Is it smooth, itchy, rough, sticky, or bumpy? Have them describe each item of clothing.

Have some materials of various textures for the children to feel and examine. These could include wool clothing (sweaters and socks), gunnysacks, rope, twine, straw, silk, satin, velvet, cotton fabric, and corduroy. With the children, talk about which fabrics or materials would make good nightgowns, sheets, pants, and so on. Most children will agree that a gunnysack would make very uncomfortable underwear and that pants woven from twine or rope might be warm, but pretty itchy! Involve the children in thinking about which things should be considered as people make and choose different materials for different pieces of clothing. What do the children think about as they look at each material? How do children feel when they look at each of the materials? How do the materials make the children feel when they touch each of the materials? For example, as the children rub the corduroy, talk with them about how people think of

corduroy as being a soft, warm material that brings a cozy feeling. You may want to read the book *Corduroy* by Don Freeman to the children and talk about this cozy little bear and his corduroy clothing.

2. **Itchy plants** Some materials look very smooth but can be very itchy! Warn children about fiberglass and plants such as poison ivy and thistles. Turn to pictures of different "itchy" plants in a plant book, and examine them with the children so they will be able to identify the plants in the future.

The Itch Book, by Crescent Dragonwagon, tells the story of an itch epidemic that hits the people in the Ozarks. The children will enjoy hearing about the people's solution to the itching. (The solution is to have a picnic and then swim in King Creek.)

From *Elephants Are Wrinkly*, published by Good Year Books. Copyright © 1997 Susan Conklin Thompson.

Our hands

1. **Read a story** Read this story to the children. Then involve the children in the activities that follow to help them appreciate how sensitive their hands are when they use them to touch.

A Small Gift

Alice rode the bus to school. It took two hours for her to get there from her hogan in the mountains. She was in the second grade at Cove Elementary School, a school on the Navajo reservation. Her mother had gone to school at Cove when the school was a large hogan and had told Alice many stories about her friends from the school. Alice liked to go to school and felt very important as she walked in the front door and walked to her room. She was learning how to read and how to spell a lot of words that she saw on signs and in books at the school.

Today, at school, there was a visitor in her classroom. A woman was sitting at the back of the room. Alice's teacher told the students that the woman was a visitor from Wyoming and that she taught people to become teachers. The woman smiled a lot, and Alice was thrilled when the woman asked her to stand with two of her friends while she took a picture. Alice forgot about the woman as she showered at the school because her family had no running water,

but she remembered to tell her mother about the woman as they cooked mutton stew over the wood stove that evening.

Three weeks later, Alice sat in her second-grade room making a felt angel to hang on the school Christmas tree. She was talking and laughing with her friends as they made the decorations. Mrs. Yazzie, the principal, walked into the room, carrying a package. She told the children that Mrs. Appletree, the woman from Wyoming who had been visiting, had sent 78 pairs of mittens, enough for each boy and girl at the school. There were red and green candy canes for each child as well. Alice's family didn't have much money, and Alice didn't often receive gifts.

Alice and her friend Kaisha each pulled on a pair of purple mittens. They laughed as they touched each other's faces. The mittens felt soft and furry on their cheeks. "I can't feel your face with this mitten on," said Alice. "I know," exclaimed Kaisha. When the bell rang to let out school, they walked outdoors, still wearing the mittens. They ran their fingers along the brick wall and picked up snow that was sheltered by the side of the building and was not whirling around from the wind. The mittens kept their hands warm, and they could not feel the bricks or the soft snow.

"Let's hurry or we'll miss the bus!" called Kaisha to her friend as they both dashed to the bus stop. Ready to start the long ride, they were still touching everything around them with their new purple mittens as they boarded the bus and the door shut behind them.

2. **Mittens and gloves** Have each child put on a pair of knit mittens and try to feel the different textures around the room. What can they feel? Why is it difficult to feel the textures with mittens on?

Help the children think about times when it is important for people to wear gloves in order to protect their hands. These times could be when people are welding, gardening, or holding animals such as raccoons or eagles.

Sometimes hands are just nice to hold, as two young girls discover in Charlotte Zolotow's book *Hold My Hand*. In this lovely book, the two girls share special winter moments as they hold each other's mittened hand.

3. **Examining our hands** The children may carefully examine the palms of their hands with a magnifying glass. Have them describe what they see. On a piece of paper, they can draw the patterns of the lines on the tips of their fingers and on their palms (they can start by drawing around their hands if this makes it easier). Explain that each person has a pattern of ridges that is different from any other person. Have each child put a small amount of poster paint on the pad of his or her index finger, then make a fingerprint by pressing his or her finger onto a piece of paper. Involve the children in carefully examining their prints.

4. **Our hands are sensitive and helpful**
The outer layer of skin on our hands is called the epidermis. This layer of skin has nerve endings that are very sensitive. Explain that this is why our hands are sensitive to hot or cold, or to objects having different textures. Talk with the children about what a privilege it is to be able to learn about the world through touch. A good book with information about your skin is called *Your Skin* by Herbert Zim.

Hands are also an important tool for communication. When people talk, they also use their hands to express themselves. Have children observe people talking and take notice of how they use their hands. Have children sit on their hands while sharing ideas. Is it difficult?

Hands are also very important for people who are hearing impaired. Ask the children

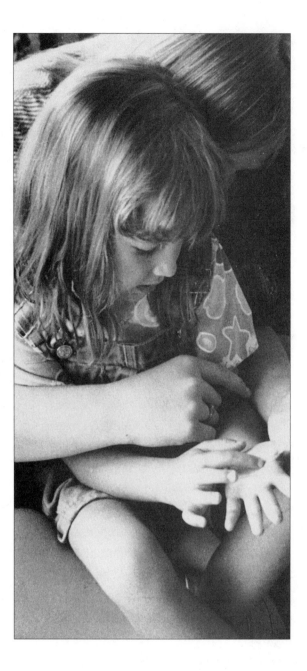

whether or not they have ever observed people talking with their hands (sign language). Many children will have observed interpreters during presentations and programs. It would be interesting for them to have a teacher of hearing impaired people, a person who is hearing impaired, or an interpreter talk to them about communicating through signs. Ada Litchfield's book *World in Our Hands* is a sensitive story about children who live with parents who are hearing impaired and is a good book to read with children as you discuss different ways people learn to communicate in the world.

Hands are also a very important communication tool for people who are visually impaired. A story about Nubia, a girl who is visually impaired, and corresponding activities are on page 42.

Chapter 5   Koalas are fuzzy

From *Elephants Are Wrinkly*, published by Good Year Books. Copyright © 1997 Susan Conklin Thompson.

Koalas are fuzzy

Integrated areas covered:

Science, Social Studies, Language Arts, and Art

From *Elephants Are Wrinkly*, published by Good Year Books. Copyright © 1997 Susan Conklin Thompson.

Activities

1. **Fuzzy wuzzy** Have a stuffed koala (or a picture of a koala) and many stuffed bears for the children to hold and squeeze. Pass them around and let the children rub them and describe how they feel. As they think of words, say them back to the children, and ask the children whether or not they know any other words that would describe how the fur feels. For example, if a child says the fur is cozy, you might say, "It is cozy. What makes it feel cozy?" The child might then say, "Because it feels warm and fuzzy." Then ask them what kind of animals these are. Most children will think that the koala is a bear. They will be surprised to know that the koala is not a bear but a marsupial!

Koalas have short fur that is fuzzy. Have the children feel their hair. Does anyone in the group think that his or her hair feels fuzzy? Which of the stuffed animals feels fuzziest?

2. **Hooking a rug** Children will really enjoy hooking a rug. A rug kit purchased in a store or a piece of rug material with various pieces of yarn and a rug hook can be placed in a center for the children to work with and then can be hung in the room. If you are working with younger children, you can hook the rug with them while they assist with matching colors, sorting yarns, and feeling the rug during its creation.

3. **Creating a koala** A koala can be created by the children using heavy paper and fuzzy materials such as stuffing, cotton, and fuzzy fabrics. Guide the children in examining the

shape of a koala, and let them cut the shape out of heavy paper. Encourage the children to choose from a selection of fuzzy materials and glue the material onto the cutout.

Buttons, felt, or pinto beans can be glued on for eyes and a nose.

4. **Padding for protection** Let the children feel the bark of several different trees. How does the bark feel? Is it smooth, rough, or bumpy? How do the various trees feel different? The bark of a weeping willow tree may feel much different from the bark of a crab apple tree. Have the children lean against the bark of a tree and describe what they feel. What does the bark look like? Are there patterns in the bark? (If there are no trees available, a brick wall would work to help children feel the rough texture.) Explain to the children that the koala's soft fuzzy fur cushions him from the hard wood of the trees. With the children, think and talk about times they have put down padding or air mattresses on the ground when they have gone camping, or put a pillow under themselves when they sat on the floor, or sat on their coats so they would not be cold from the sidewalk, step, or floor. Those are times it would be very helpful to have padding on our bodies like the koalas have on theirs. Then place a pillow or blanket (folded into a square) against the tree and have the children lean against the tree again. Now have them describe what they feel. How does it feel different with the padding?

The fuzzy fur also works as a ladder for the baby koala. He crawls out of the pouch up to his mother's head by grabbing onto the fuzzy fur. They have very sharp claws that help them crawl. The koala is certainly not as cuddly as it looks! Let the children discuss different animals they have seen that look cuddly but are not. (See the story *The New Kittens* on pages 26–28.)

More information about koalas

- *Koalas live in the forests in Australia.*
- *Koalas live in, and eat leaves from, eucalyptus trees.*
- *The San Diego Zoo is one of the few zoos that has koalas because eucalyptus trees can be grown in San Diego's climate.*
- *Baby koalas are born without any fur and are only as big as a small mouse or child's thumb.*
- *Like other marsupials, the baby koala lives in its mother's pouch until it is big enough to crawl onto her fur and ride on her back (at the age of about six months).*
- *Koalas eat all night and sleep all day. They leave the tree only in order to move to another tree.*
- *Koalas don't drink much water but get most of the moisture they need from eating tree leaves.*

Resources on koalas

Koalas Live Here, by Iberle Irmengarde
The Koala, by Carl Green and William R. Sanford
Koalas, by Patricia Hunt
Australian Marsupials, by Peter Crowcroft

From *Elephants Are Wrinkly,* published by Good Year Books. Copyright © 1997 Susan Conklin Thompson.

Extension

Feeding animal babies All babies in nature need lots of care. Ask the children to think and talk about the kinds of care babies need. One need that baby animals have is to be fed. Lead the children in discussing a specific animal and what they know about how its mother or father feeds it. For example, many children will have seen a mother bird bringing worms to its babies. A baby koala starts out drinking milk from its mother when it is in the pouch. When the baby is old enough to crawl out of the pouch, it learns how to eat leaves by watching its mother. Talk with the children about the similarities between human babies and mammalian animal babies, such as they both first drink milk and then move to other liquids and solids.

Some animals are separated from their mothers, or their mothers will not feed them. Louie, an elephant trainer (see story, page 10), raised a baby elephant because its mother did not understand how to raise her baby. He fed the baby elephant with a milk bottle until it was old enough to eat solid food. In the story *Charlotte's Web* by E. B. White, Wilbur the pig is also fed with a milk bottle until he can eat from a dish.

Koalas and transportation

Activities

1. ***Transporting babies*** Koalas carry their babies around first in a pouch and then on their backs. The older babies ride piggy-back. Explain to the children that other animals carry their babies a variety of ways. A kangaroo also has a pouch, a beaver picks up a baby with its front legs and carries it like a human would, a baby swan sits on its mother's back as she swims along, a crocodile carries its babies in its mouth, and other animals such as raccoons and cats pick up their babies using their teeth to grab the baby's skin at the back of its neck.

How do people transport their young? Discuss with the children various ways they have seen people transporting their children. Have a stroller, a car seat, and some type of pack available for the children to examine (and any other pieces of equipment for carrying children). Let the children strap or place a doll into the carriers and transport the doll across the room and back.

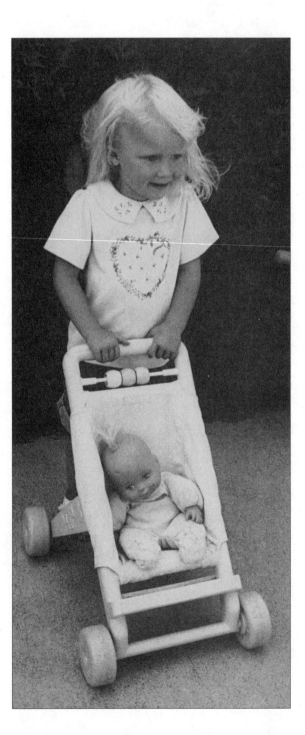

2. *Getting children from here to there*

Have a picture of a cradle board available for the children to see. Explain how people in

various cultures have used everything from baskets to cradle boards to carry their babies. American Indians used to place a baby in a cradle board to carry him or her for long distances. Modern-day baby packs are a lot like these original cradle boards.

Women in Central and South America tie their babies to their backs with a shawl-like piece of material. This is a woman in Guatemala, carrying her baby like a marsupial! It stays close to her body and certainly looks very cozy. The piece of material used is common to outfits in Central and South America. It can be used to wrap a bundle to be carried on top of the head, or folded differently to carry a baby.

With a long piece of material, demonstrate
how to fold the material and use it to tie a
baby onto your back. The children can
experiment with tying and carrying a doll on
their backs. They can take the piece of
material, fold it into a hat, and place it on
their heads. They will be interested in
thinking about how one piece of material
can be used for many things.

As you talk about how different animals and
people carry their babies, teach the children
the following song.

Babies Are Carried in Many Different Ways

From *Elephants Are Wrinkly*, published by Good Year Books. Copyright © 1997 Susan Conklin Thompson.

Koalas and extinction

Activities

1. **Saving the koala** Have several pieces of fuzzy or furry clothing available for the children to feel, try on, or rub on their skin. Explain to them that this fur is similar to the cozy fur of the koala and that at one time, many koalas were being killed for their fur. Also, farmers were cutting down many of the koalas' trees, and the koalas had fewer places to live and less to eat. Forest fires were also destroying their forests. Because of these three things, fewer and fewer koalas were able to survive.

Tell the children that Australian boys and girls, like themselves, loved the koalas and were concerned about them. The children worried that eventually there would not be any koalas left; they would be extinct. Explain to children that koalas had become an endangered species. Thousands of boys and girls planted eucalyptus trees in their yards and when the trees were strong enough, the children gave them to forest rangers who put them in special areas that were set aside to protect the koalas. After a while koalas were no longer in danger of becoming extinct.

There are many species of animals that are endangered. Talk with the children about how important it is to learn more about animals so we know how to take care of them and provide for their needs so they will not become extinct. (Refer to the story "Tammy Batson: A Zookeeper," page 36.)

2. **Eucalyptus tree collage** Children can tear construction paper into small pieces to create a eucalyptus tree collage.

Marsupials and pockets

Activities

1. **Animals with pockets** Kangaroos are also marsupials. Marsupials carry their babies in their pouches until the babies become old enough to be on the outside. Other marsupials include opossums, wombats, and bandicoots. A pocket keeps a marsupial baby warm and secure. When the baby marsupials are born, they are very tiny and have no hair. They immediately crawl into their mother's pouch and stay there. These pouches are almost like a pocket. Each animal in nature has a home that is well suited for it.

2. **Everyday pockets** The children will be interested in thinking about a pocket being a home for a small marsupial. Ask the children whether or not they think that is how people got the idea for a pocket. Of course, our pockets are not homes for babies but do come in quite handy! The children can wear or bring something to school that has a pocket. Encourage them to bring in some unusual items to share, along with sweatshirts and other pieces of clothing. Then have the children share their pockets— everything from pockets in a book to pockets in shoes! As the children show their pockets, they can tell what the pocket is used for. When they are done, brainstorm as a group some other pockets you could invent that would be handy.

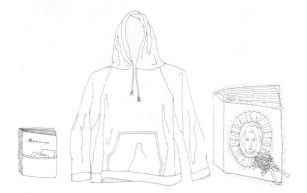

3. **Discovery game** Wear an apron that has several pockets. In each pocket, place an object so that it is out of sight from the children. See whether or not the children can guess what is in each pocket. You could give them a clue about the texture and allow them to ask questions with yes or no answers. For example, you might place a piece of cotton into a pocket. You can tell the children that it is very soft. Let them ask questions and make guesses until they get it correct. The children will also enjoy being the ones to wear the apron. After the children catch on to the game, help a child tie on the apron, peek into the pocket so he or she will be able to answer the questions about the item, and then let the other children guess what is in the pocket.

What do children put into pockets? Read the following story to the children. Then involve them in talking about things they put into their pockets.

4. **Read a story** Read this short story to children and then involve them in the activities that follow.

What's in a Pocket?

Hannah was excited to get home. She watched the dark sky out of the car window as she rode to her house from the ballet recital. Her sister Kallie was still moving her arms in dance motions as they rode along.

As soon as the car stopped, Kallie and Hannah jumped out the door and ran into the front yard. "Oh, Kallie!" her mother exclaimed. "You are getting your tutu all dirty!" Kallie barely looked at her mother as she and Hannah stuck their hands into the soft, gooey dirt of the garden. They were looking for worms. It had been raining all day and now the sky was dark and clear. The light from the porch shone on the garden, and they could spot the plump worms slithering through the dark, damp earth.

Kallie's mother scooped her up to take her inside to change her clothes. Hannah was relieved that she had on overalls instead of that silly tutu that itched her arms when she laid them at her sides. She took the plastic shovel and carefully separated a worm from the dirt. Then she grabbed the wriggly worm and held it in her hand, close to her face, examining it before she dropped it into her pocket.

Then Mom came out to get Hannah. "Into the tub with you," she said as she scooped her up and carried her into the bathroom.

From *Elephants Are Wrinkly*, published by Good Year Books. Copyright © 1997 Susan Conklin Thompson.

"Let's empty your pockets, Hannah, before we take your overalls off. Your pockets look pretty lumpy."

Hannah stuck a small hand into a pocket and pulled out a rough, gray rock. She placed it carefully on a chair. Then she put her hand in again and pulled out several more rocks, which she put next to the first rock. After the rocks, out came six small pinecones from the pine tree in the front yard, two plastic bottle caps, seven small sticks, a broken and sticky piece of a lollipop, a small ball, pieces of partly squashed cereal from her breakfast, a small blue hair bow, some squashed yellow dandelion tops, and at the bottom, squiggling all around, was one long, plump worm.

"Yuck!" exclaimed Hannah's mom. "Live things don't belong in your pocket, Hannah! They will die if you take them out of their environment."

"Not if I were a koala or a kangaroo," laughed Hannah. "Then I could carry around my babies in my pocket. But I guess worms are different, huh Mom?"

"Yes, Hannah, worms are different," said Hannah's mom. "Now into the tub with you, and after your bath I'll take this worm back to its home, the garden."

"I have to get clean, but the worm can get dirty in the garden. I wonder why worms are so lucky," sighed Hannah as she stepped gingerly into the water.

In this story, the pocket was not a good home for the worm. Lead the children in talking about wild creatures and their environments. It is important that children realize that although it may be interesting to bring a small creature into their home, they should return it to its natural environment shortly. Point out how Hannah's mother took the worm back to the garden because it needed to be in its own home, or environment, in order to live.

5. **Make a pocket** Make a big paper pocket out of colored butcher paper. Staple it around the edge and hang it on the wall. Select a theme to use for what's in the pocket. For example, you may want to use the theme of Tools. Each child can make a paper tool and place it in the pocket. On his or her tool, the child can write about what the tool is and how it is used (the children can use invented spelling). He or she might draw a picture of someone using the tool or write a poem about it on the paper tool. Then, when all of the children have placed their objects into the pocket, remove the tools one at a time, and share and discuss them with the group. Other themes might be Foods Children Like, Animals/Pets, Flowers, Favorite Book Characters, and Self-portraits.

Read Rebecca Caudill's book *A Pocketful of Cricket* and talk with the children about the interesting things Jay had in his pocket—even a cricket that goes with him to school!

Fuzzy fruits and vegetables

1. **A peach is fuzzy** Have an assortment of fruits and vegetables for the children to examine. Possibilities include a coconut, an ear of corn, kiwis, peaches, apricots, a pineapple, an apple, a green pepper, an avocado, and a potato. Encourage the children to feel and carefully observe each one. What shapes and colors are the fruits and vegetables? The children can estimate size by such comments as "the apple looks about the size of an adult's fist." Different pieces of fruits and vegetables can actually be measured using a soft tape measure, and the size can be compared and contrasted. Then let them talk about the textures. Which fruits and vegetables feel fuzzy? Of these, which are the fuzziest? How about the ones that don't feel fuzzy, what do they feel like? If the children were going to compare the vegetables' and fruits' textures to animals, which animals would they be like? For example, the coconut is shaggy like the camel, the husk on the ear of corn is smooth and layered like the feathers on the flamingo, but the corn silk is shaggy like the camel, and the pineapple feels prickly like a porcupine (but not nearly as sharp).

From *Elephants Are Wrinkly*, published by Good Year Books. Copyright © 1997 Susan Conklin Thompson.

The children can group or order the fruits and vegetables according to texture. They can also make patterns with the produce.

If you live close to a field, park, or orchard where fruits and vegetables are grown, it is very interesting to go there on a "field" trip and actually feel the cornstalks and corn, pumpkins, apples, and other produce. A trip in the fall, one in the winter, and another in the spring and/or summer will help children view nature's cycles and provide a greater understanding of the sights, smells, and textures of different seasons.

The Seasons of Arnold's Apple Tree, by Gail Gibbons, shows nature's cycles through the way the seasons affect an apple tree, and is a nice book to share with children.

2. **Sketching a still life** Make a still life arrangement with the fruits and vegetables. Let the children practice drawing the shapes or painting the arrangements. Involve the children in arranging the fruits and vegetables into different configurations. Show the children a famous print of a fruit or vegetable still life such as one by Vincent Van Gogh.

Talk with them about the colors in the painting, the objects, how the painting makes them feel, and other areas the children may be interested in discussing.

3. **What else is fuzzy?** Peaches, apricots, and kiwis are fuzzy. Ask the children to think about what else is fuzzy. Fill a pillow sack or grocery bag with items that are fuzzy and nonfuzzy. These might include fuzzy slippers, earmuffs, stuffed animals, and pajamas with feet. In the bag, also include items that are not fuzzy. Have each child in turn pull an item from the bag for the class to examine. Classify the object as fuzzy or not fuzzy.

4. **A trip to the grocery store** A trip to a food market or produce aisle in a grocery store is a feast for young children's senses! Have them go on a texture hunt, finding something that is rough, something that is

short booklet for each child with a different heading on each page (rough, soft, bumpy, fuzzy, smooth, sticky, prickly). Let the store manager know that you will be going on a texture hunt. When you get to the market, the children can carefully feel the different items and see which ones will be appropriate for each page. As they find the items, have them draw the vegetable or fruit and briefly describe it. When you get back to the room or home, encourage them to color in the fruits and vegetables and to add to their descriptions. With the children, make a large class book and combine the children's items.

The Guatemalan market above is colorful, busy, and filled with many textures!

5. **Estimating plants** Some natural materials are also fuzzy. A dandelion that is ready to release its seeds into the wind is fuzzy. Show one to the children or have an illustration of one they can see. They will be interested in thinking about how the seeds leave the fuzzy dandelion and spread themselves around in their environment. The children can take turns blowing small puffs of air into the dandelion and observing what happens. Hold the dandelion over a piece of paper so the children can see what happens to the seeds when they blow. The children may also take a dandelion seed outside in a slight

breeze and watch to see which direction it travels, how long it floats in the air, and what happens to it as it drifts to the ground. Milkweeds also will work well for this activity.

A warm fuzzy

Activities

1. **Blankets and fuzzy things** Hand the children several cozy blankets to cuddle. Ask them how the blanket feels. How does it make them feel when they hug it? We call this a warm fuzzy. Ask the children to talk about what makes them feel good and warm inside. Have a special day when the children can bring a blanket or a stuffed animal or something else that makes them feel good and warm inside. Let them share items with their classmates.

2. **A group poem** As a group, examine the warm, fuzzy items the children brought from home. Talk with the children about how things that we like can make us feel warm and fuzzy, and so can things that people do for us or say to us. Even things like being warm in the house on a rainy day can make us feel cozy. As a group, write a poem about different things that the children think of as being warm fuzzies. As each child contributes a line, write it on a chart or board

while the children watch. A poem might look like this:

A warm fuzzy

Marshmallows floating in my hot chocolate
My dog Charlie giving me a kiss
Hugging my grandma
  Sleeping with Raggedy Ann
When my dad tells me I am a good helper
My sister reading me a book
Making cookies with my stepmother
When Carrie saves me a place at the
  lunch table
Jumping rope with my friends
Sitting on the step in the sun
Growing plants in my garden

3. **Warm fuzzies and cold pricklies** Talk with the children about things they say or do to give a warm fuzzy to someone else. Encourage them to talk about what they say or do for their friends and families that makes those people feel good. Ask them to think about how they themselves feel when they make others feel good.

Take out some cold, whole dill pickles and put them on a plate. Pass around the plate of pickles and let the children feel the textures. What do the pickles feel like? With a knife, cut different pickles into small pieces and give each child one to taste. Talk with them about the tart taste. Then ask them, "What do you think it means when someone talks about a cold prickly?" Encourage them to think and talk about how the pickle felt cold and kind of prickly, and that some things can make us feel warm and fuzzy but other things can make us feel cold and prickly. Give the children a chance to talk about some things that make them feel cold and prickly inside.

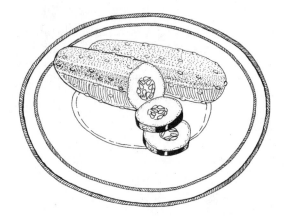

Chapter 6   Camels are shaggy

 Camels are shaggy

Animals for travel and packing

Water and you

Humpy lumps

From shaggy dogs to carpets

Shaggy hair and you

Camels are shaggy

Integrated areas covered:

Science, Social Studies, Language Arts, Art, and Music

Activities

1. ***Shaggy materials*** Which things are shaggy? Involve children in thinking about different things they have seen that are shaggy. Have shaggy objects available for them to feel, such as moss hanging from a tree or a shaggy piece of fur or items that look shaggy, such as shredded newspaper. The children can feel the shaggy materials and describe what they see and feel. Challenge them to find some material at home or in the outside environment that seems shaggy. When they bring in the shaggy materials, let the children feel and describe them, sort them, and make labels for them, such as ones that are mossy or others that are like a rug.

Have a model or a picture of a camel for the children to examine (see page 87 for resources). Involve the children in looking carefully at the pictures of the camels and discussing what they see. Some camels have one hump (dromedary camels), and others have two humps (bactrian camels). The bactrian camels are the shaggiest. As children look at the model or picture, have them point out where the shaggiest hair is on the camel.

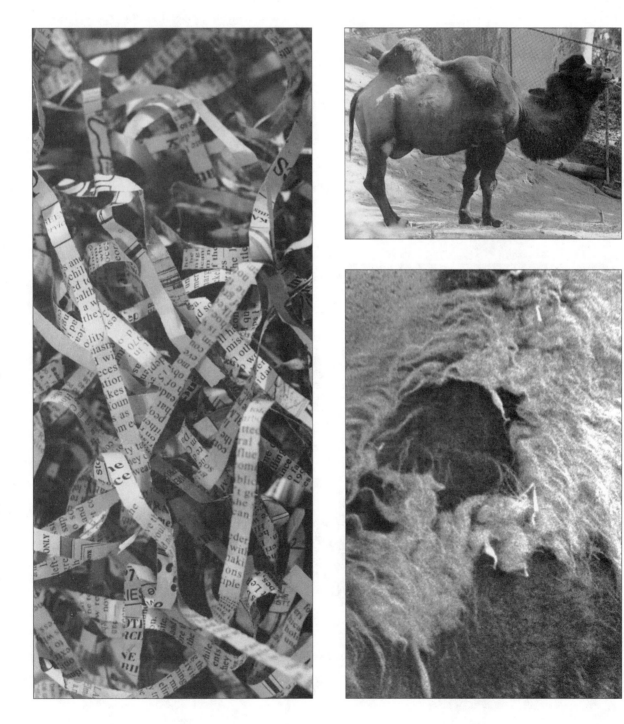

2. **Creating a shaggy camel** Out of butcher paper, cut an outline of a large camel. The children can glue or tape their shaggy materials onto the paper camel. Remind them that the camel is shaggiest on the top of its humps, legs, head, and above and below the neck.

3. **What comes from a camel?** Tell the children that the camels lose most of this shaggy hair (or their coats) when spring comes and they no longer need it for warmth. New hair grows underneath this coat. The hair closest to the camel's skin is silky and is used to make blankets, sweaters, cloth, and sometimes tents in the countries where they live. The outside hair is coarse and is used for ropes and rugs. If you have something made from camel hair, let the children examine the item.

Ask the children whether or not they know what color camels are. They will be interested and surprised to know that this tan color is called "camel"! What else can the children name that is this color?

More information about camels

‣ *Camels have huge feet that can walk on top of sand without sinking in.*
‣ *Camels are used to carry heavy loads, and the word* camel *means "to carry a burden."*

- *People ride camels and sit right on the hump or between two humps!*
- *Camels can measure up to seven feet tall and weigh about 1,200 pounds.*
- *Camels eat only plants and have a split upper lip so they can get their teeth close to the ground in order to get to short grass.*
- *Some camels can go months without water in cool weather, and up to a week during dry, hot days.*
- *The camel's hump is a large lump of fat (weighing up to one hundred pounds), and if a camel cannot find food, it can live off this fat for a while.*

Resources on camels

Camel, by Caroline Arnold

Camels, by John Thompson

Camels and Llamas, by Olive Earle

CAMELS

Extensions

1. **A camel's foot** Fill a box with sand or go outside to a sand pile. Have each child push a finger into the sand as hard as he or she can. Then have each child make a fist and try to push it into the sand. What happens? Give each child a sturdy, plastic plate to place on the sand. Have the child push down on the plate. Now what happens? Help the children explore through observing and discussing what happens when they push a finger, then a fist, and finally a plate into the sand. Explain to them that a camel's foot can be as big as a plate and, just like the plate they used, it is hard to push into the sand because of its wide surface. Involve them in thinking of animals that have narrow feet (such as goats) and how they would sink more easily into the sand, as did children's fingers.

2. **Song and movement** Using a sash or strip of material, help children tie pillows onto their backs. Then involve them in the following song.

From *Elephants Are Wrinkly*, published by Good Year Books. Copyright © 1997 Susan Conklin Thompson.

I'm a Camel with a Hump

I'm a cam- el with a hump; Watch me go "bump", "bump"; Two steps for- ward, take a jump and turn a- round.

Fine

1. I walk on the hot and dust- y
2. I stop at the wa- ter hole and

D.C. al Fine

sand; As I car- ry my mas- ter 'cross the land.
drink; And I turn to my ne- igh- bor and wink.

88

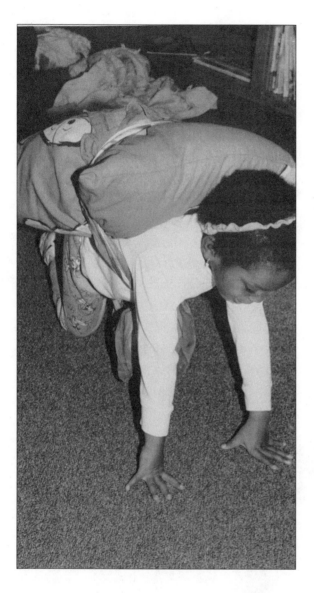

sides to the sun. Let the children experiment with this outside. Have them face the sun and feel how much of their bodies receives the rays. Then have them turn sideways to the sun and discuss how less of their bodies is exposed. Caution them not to look at the sun because of the sensitive nature of their eyes. To explore further what has been warmed by the sun, have them feel surfaces such as different parts of the sidewalk, walls of a building, and bike tires. Encourage them to discuss how the different surfaces feel. Which ones feel hot, cool, or cold? Does the warmth of the surface have anything to do with its color? Use a thermometer and graph the temperatures.

3. **Warmth from the sun** Camels' bodies appear very broad when viewed from the side and very thin when viewed from the front. A camel can face the broad side of its body toward the sun and get warm, or if he needs to cool down, he can turn his head and body to face the sun and keep most of his body out of the rays. This is different from when children face the sun. When they face the sun, more of their bodies catch the rays than when they turn their

Animals for travel and packing

1. *How many pounds can a camel carry?*

Camels are often used for carrying loads from one location to another. Bactrian camels sometimes carry as much as one thousand pounds! Supplies are loaded onto a camel when it is sitting down, and the camel will not stand up if the load is too heavy or is loaded in a way in which it is difficult to carry. Lift something heavy onto a table. A bag of dog food or feed that weighs about ten pounds would work well. As you lift the bag, talk to the children about how you are lifting the weight with your legs so

you will not strain your back. The children can also try lifting the bag if it is under ten pounds (be careful about asking them to lift something that is too heavy because they may strain their muscles). Then have the children figure out how many ten pound bags a camel would carry if it was carrying one thousand pounds.

Camels are also fun for children if they can get on and catch a ride!

2. ***Llamas versus camels*** Show the children a picture of a llama. Hold it up next to a picture of a camel and have the children discuss what they observe about the two animals that is the same, and what they observe that is different. Llamas are related to camels but have no humps. They are also commonly used as pack animals, especially in Peru. Explain to the children that they belong to the same animal family ("camelid"). Have them think about their own families. How are some of the people the same and how are they different? Do they share characteristics with anyone in their families? When camels and llamas are

disturbed, they spit an unpleasant liquid. With people, it is considered impolite and very unsanitary to spit at people or things. Explain to the children that their saliva helps them to taste, but that it contains many germs that can make other people sick.

Read aloud the book *Is Your Mama a Llama?* by Deborah Guarino and talk with children about different characteristics the animals in the book have.

3. ***Horses and oxen*** Other animals such as horses and oxen also pull wagons and carry supplies. Have the children discuss that even today we use horses to pull wagons and carts. Sometimes we see them pulling fancy carts and old ice wagons in parades. Oxen were very helpful on the farm for plowing and pulling wagons and in some places are still used for these jobs today.

4. ***Ways we carry things*** Do people carry things on their backs like camels do? Have the children think about how people carry things from one place to another. They use paper sacks, backpacks, baskets, and other containers. How do children get their items to school? Many children will have a backpack or other type of bag. Ask them why they use what they do. How about when they take a trip? What do they use? When they go to the grocery store, how do they carry home the groceries? Talk with them about how some people bring permanent bags or pillow cases to carry their items home so they can save on bags or sacks. Have the children ask a grocer how many sacks are given out each day. Of these, how many are plastic and how many are paper? How many people bring their own sacks? Make a "bag" graph with this information. How can we reuse the sacks we get at the store? How about the ones in which the children may bring their lunches?

From *Elephants Are Wrinkly*, published by Good Year Books. Copyright © 1997 Susan Conklin Thompson.

5. **Packing a suitcase** Ahead of time, carefully pack a suitcase for a short trip. Have a child unpack the suitcase one item at a time, and have him or her discuss each item as it is removed. Bring the class's attention to how you folded the sweater carefully so it would not wrinkle and you packed it because you knew the evenings would be cool. You may want to close the suitcase after each item to give each child a turn. As you go along, include each child in anticipating what is in the suitcase. When a child is getting ready to remove the toothpaste, you might comment, "I wonder what is in here to clean my teeth?" Leave the suitcase in an area of the room where different children can practice packing and unpacking it.

6. **How many items fit in a backpack?**

A pack is placed on a camel when the camel is lying down. If the pack is too heavy, the camel will not stand up. How many items can go in a pack that a person puts on? Lay an empty backpack on a table. Next to the backpack, place a large number of items, such as a flashlight, socks, a shirt, and an apple. Ask the children to estimate how many items can go into the backpack. Record their guesses on a chart or the board.

Next tell the children that they are going to take part in an experiment. Explain to them that you are wondering whether or not different children can pack the items in different ways, so that some children can fit more

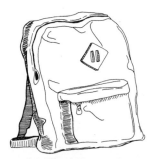

items into the pack than others. Ask them to guess whether or not some children can fit more items into the pack because of how they place the items in the pack. Explain to them that where you put items in a pack is important. You usually put heavy items and hard items at the bottom and light or breakable items on the top.

Let children take turns packing the pack and then taking out the items as other children count them. On the chart or board, record the number of tries and how many items were packed. Have the children set a rule on what is considered a full pack so items are not spilling out all over. When you are ready to end the activity, have the children help you draw a line to create a simple graph of how many children packed the bag and how many items each child packed. Then have the children weigh the pack. Would this pack be too heavy for a child to carry?

Water and you

Activities

1. **Foods contain water** Camels can get most of the water they need by eating food, such as grass, that has a lot of moisture in it. Talk with the children about foods they eat (such as celery and carrots) that have moisture in them. Look at the photo at right. Do they think these are enough carrots to feed a camel?

2. **Measuring and graphing liquids**
Camels can go for about six months in cool weather without drinking any liquid. Ask the children what they drink during the day. How often do they drink a liquid? Explain that they should drink 6–8 cups of water each day to keep their bodies healthy. Have them keep track for one or two days of how many times they drink and what they drink. Have the children graph the different liquids and how many times they drank each liquid.

When camels do drink, they drink huge amounts of water at one time. A grown camel can drink about fifty gallons of water in one day. Have a gallon jug for the children to fill with water. Have the children draw fifty jugs on the board or make fifty marks to indicate how many gallons a camel can drink. Count them with the children.

Ask the children how much they can drink at one time. Collect one-gallon milk containers until you have fifty. How much space do fifty gallons take up? Have children guess how heavy fifty gallons would be?

It's lucky for the camel that it can go a long time without water because it is difficult to find water in a desert, and the camel has no way to store it to drink later. Encourage the children to talk about ways they store water or other liquids in the refrigerator. Have them think about taking a walk or a hike. How could they take water with them? How could they carry the containers so the containers do not get too heavy on the trip?

3. **How much liquid does a container hold?** Have a variety of containers for the children to examine. Include such containers as a glass jar, bucket, thermos, canteen, pitcher, and jug. Have the children help you put water in each container. Ask them to predict which container will hold the most water, the next largest amount, and so on. Using a measuring cup, fill the containers. As the children pour the liquid in, help them help them record how many cupfuls are going into each container. When all the containers are full, the children can order them according to amount of water. They will probably be surprised at how much some containers can hold, and which containers hold the most. Talk with the children about how it is difficult sometimes to tell from only its shape which container will hold the most. For example, the tallest one may not hold as much as the shortest one because the short one may be wider.

Humpy lumps

Activities

1. **Lumps and humps** Camels need to have a hump to store their fat, which they may draw on later for food as they need it. Some camels have two humps, and children like themselves ride between the humps. Ask the children to think about the camel's humps. What if the camel had a lump instead of a hump? What is the difference between a lump and a hump?

Ask the children whether or not they have ever made their beds. Have a child demonstrate what he or she does to make a bed. Is his or her bed ever lumpy? Ask the children if they think a lump is different from a hump. How?

Have available a blanket, pillow, stuffed animal, sock, shoe, marble, and other small items. Let the children take turns putting items under the blanket and then discussing whether the items made a hump, lump, or even a bump. Can they describe the differences between the humps, lumps, or bumps made by the different items? If one of the children gets under the blanket, would this be a lump or a bump?

Read the humorous book *The Cowboy and the Black-Eyed Pea*, by Tony Johnston and Warren Ludwig. This is a very clever story similar to the "Princess and the Pea," only it is about a cowboy. The black-eyed pea does not create a hump, but makes a lump so uncomfortable that the cowboy can hardly ride his horse. The picture on the next page was created by first- and second-graders after they had read this story. Notice how many saddle blankets there are and the patterns on each!

2. **Lumpy pudding** Make a pudding mix with the children. Before they beat it smooth, have them look at the lumps. Encourage them to discuss other foods that they have made or eaten that are lumpy, such as oatmeal. Ask them whether or not they have ever eaten food that is humpy or bumpy.

4. ***Animal cookies*** For a fun and tasty learning session, give each child a small box of animal crackers. Guide them in pouring the cookies onto a paper plate and then examining each animal. Can they find a camel profile on a cookie? Some brands of boxes will include camels while others will not. Which animals are in the boxes? Lead the children in grouping the different animals together. How many animals are in each box? How many different kinds of animals are in the boxes? When the children group the animals into types or sets, how many are in each set? Working with items such as cookies provides a good opportunity to talk with children about the position of one object in relation to another. For example, you might ask the children to lay out the animals and then tell which animal is above the camel, next to the camel, and so on. (A nicely illustrated book to share with children about positions of objects is *Over, Under, and Through*, by Tana Hoban.) The children may then eat the tasty cookies.

3. ***Ships of the desert*** Camels have been called "ships of the desert" because of their profile with their humps, and because like ships they are used to carry freight. Encourage the children to discuss why camels are compared to ships. If you have a small model or a photograph of a profile of a ship, lay it next to the one of the camel so the children can make comparisons between the two.

From shaggy dogs to carpets

Activities

1. **Shaggy animals** Which other animals have shaggy hair like a camel? Ask the children this question and challenge them to bring to school a picture of an animal that has shaggy hair. These might be pictures of a pet that they have, ones they cut out of a magazine, or ones they might draw. Display the pictures and discuss them with the children. Allow time for each child to talk about the picture he or she brought.

2. **Shaggy hair care** How do you take care of a pet with shaggy hair? Have a veterinarian, his or her assistant, a pet-store owner, or someone else that grooms animals come and talk to the children about caring for an animal's coat. You may want to take the children to his or her office or shop to do this.

3. **Molting**   The camel molts (loses its shaggy coat) in the spring because it does not need the hair to keep it warm after the winter is over. Talk with the children about other animals that molt, such as dogs, deer, horses, bighorn sheep, and elk. Sheep would molt, but we usually shear them in the early spring for their wool.

Ask the children whether or not their hair keeps their bodies warm in the spring. What do they do so they are not cold when the temperatures are low? What do they remove in the spring, or "molt," so they do not become overheated?

Ask the children to think about how their lives would be different if they had shaggy hair all over like a camel and did not have to wear clothing for warmth. Would they still need to go to the mall? What would happen at school when they began to molt? When they took a bath, would their hair clog up the drain? They will enjoy drawing or paint-

4. ***How much shag does a carpet have?***
Have a variety of carpet samples available for the children to examine. A local carpet store should be able to furnish you with samples of carpets with different naps. Be sure to include some that are a long shag. The children can rub their hands over the various pieces of carpet. How does it feel? Do some carpets feel different? How? The children can then order the carpets from the shortest nap to the longest.

Talk with the children about carpet in their homes. What kinds of carpet do they have? What colors are the carpets in their homes? What colors might hide dirt and stains? For what other reasons do children think people choose the carpets that they do?

5. ***Design a room*** Using pieces of carpet remnants, let each child take a box and design a room that would coordinate with the carpet. The carpet can be laid or taped (using two-sided tape) inside the bottom of the boxes. Children can find wallpaper samples (sample books of wallpaper are given away at most wallpaper or paint stores) that match the carpet. They can make furniture, add pictures to the walls, and make other interesting things for their rooms.

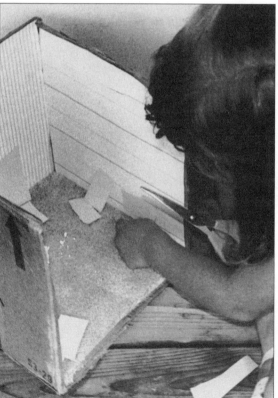

Shaggy hair and you

Activities

1. **Read a story** Read this short story to children and then involve them in the activities that follow.

Shaggy Maggi

Maggi woke up on Tuesday morning with a throat that felt scratchy, a nose that would not breathe like it was supposed to, and eyes that felt watery and burned. She dragged herself out to the breakfast table and told her dad how she was feeling. "No kindergarten for you today," said her dad. "You will have to come to the shop with me."

Maggi thought that would be okay. She did not get to go to the shop very often with her dad because there was a sign above the desk that asked moms and dads not to bring their children with them when they came. Maggi grabbed her coat and followed her dad out the door.

Maggi loved to read, but sitting in a red plastic chair in the corner of the shop she could see all around her, so she put her book on the floor and watched the different customers. Some were tall, some were short, some were women, and some were men. They all came to have either their hair cut, their fingernails taken care of, or both.

It was busy in the shop. Lots of people were talking, walking back and forth getting supplies, and answering the phone. Maggi was mostly watching her father cut hair at the booth in front of her. Scissors were clipping quickly and brown hair was falling in long strands on the floor. Maggi thought the lady getting her hair cut was probably making a mistake. Her long brown hair looked nice hanging around her face, but her father was cutting it off and it was looking kind of like Moe's, her friend's scraggly brown dog that was at the dog pound for an entire month before her friend discovered her and took her home.

The man next to Maggi had some very shaggy hair. It hung to his shoulders and was pretty wild from his last permanent. Maggi was reminded of the lion in her picture book, the one with the shaggy mane. She also thought about the camel that was in the book because it was shaggy and had lots of hunks of brown hair falling partly off. Her mom said that was called molting and lots of hairy animals like camels and buffalo molt. Maggi thought it looked odd having that hair falling off, but her sister Rosy said camels were real characters so they were supposed to look odd.

Maggi looked back at the lady and her dad. Shorter and shorter the brown hair became as her dad clipped. The lady was talking on and on about her niece, her cats, and everything else that had happened in the last ten years, thought Maggi. Pretty soon the lady in the chair quit looking like Moe. Her hair was getting shorter and shorter. "Fuzzy Wuzzy was a bear, Fuzzy Wuzzy had no hair," thought Maggi.

Maggi was reminded of the animals they were learning about in kindergarten. On the bulletin board, they had a big picture of a koala and her baby, which was riding on her back. Both of them were cute and looked very fuzzy. They had small black eyes that looked out at you from the picture. There was also a picture of a kangaroo that was fuzzy and had babies, only you couldn't see the babies because they were inside the pouch. Next to the kangaroo was a picture of a bear, and it also looked fuzzy, a lot like the lady's hair.

"Beautiful!" exclaimed her dad as he turned the chair and handed the lady a small hand mirror to look in. The lady made a pleasant sound and handed back the mirror. Then

her dad took off the cape and shook out the hair. Both of them looked pleased.

"How does it look, Maggi?" asked Dad, smiling. "She looks like she could be on a poster, doesn't she?" Maggi almost laughed as she said, "That's just what I was thinking."

2. **Hair changes** Involve the children in discussing this story. What did they think the shop was going to be? You may want to stop part way into the story and have them predict where Maggi is going. Then let them share the experiences they have had going to a beauty shop, a barber shop, or at home having a family member cut their hair.

Ask the children whether or not their hair has changed since they were babies. Their hair may have changed color and become more, or less, curly. Encourage them to bring in baby pictures to look at as a group. What other physical features have changed since they were babies?

3. **Clay hair on clay heads** Have several mirrors available for children to examine their reflections. Each child can look into a mirror and describe his or her face and hair (in writing or orally with a friend). Using a small hunk of potter's clay (purchased at ceramic stores), have each child model a head with a face that looks like him or her. They will love making hair for their clay heads by pressing a small lump of clay through a garlic press, then arranging and attaching the clay hair pieces by pressing the ends of the strands onto the head.

4. **Pick your style** At some beauty salons and stores, they can take a picture of a person, put the image in a computer and let the person put many different hairstyles around his or her face until he or she finds an attractive one. Give each child a plain sheet of paper. He or she can draw many different circles to resemble faces on the sheet, and try drawing and coloring different hairstyles around the circles. Provide the children time to discuss how the various hairstyles give each face a different look.

From *Elephants Are Wrinkly*, published by Good Year Books. Copyright © 1997 Susan Conklin Thompson.

Chapter 7 Anteaters have sticky tongues

Jen & Des Bartlett / Photo Researchers

 Anteaters have sticky tongues

Your tongue

Sticky situations

Pet day

Sticky in nature

Anteaters have sticky tongues

Integrated areas covered:
Science, Social Studies, Language Arts,
Math, Art, and Music

Activities

1. ***What is sticky?*** Ahead of time, pour a small amount of clear corn syrup onto a small plate. Don't tell the children that the syrup is on the plate, and hold the plate slightly above their view. Take a glass with a flat bottom and ask them what they think will happen if you place the glass on the plate. They will probably answer that the glass will rest on the plate. Place the glass on the plate, resting it on the corn syrup. Hold onto the glass with one hand and the plate with another. Ask them what they think will happen if you take your hand off the plate but hold onto the glass. Most children will say that the plate will fall down. When you take your hand away, the plate will stay stuck to the glass by the syrup. When something happens differently from what we expect, it is called a discrepant event. Discrepant events can be very motivating for children as they think about why and how things happen. Ask the children why they think the plate stayed with the glass. After they are done sharing their ideas, show them the syrup on the plate. Let them touch the syrup and feel how sticky it is. What else is sticky?

2. ***Anteaters' sticky tongues*** Anteaters have sticky tongues. Ask the children whether or not they have ever seen an anteater. Why do they think these animals are called anteaters? Show them a model and/or picture of an anteater. What do they observe? Explain to them that anteaters eat termites, ants, and soft-bodied grubs. Anteaters have very sharp claws that they use to tear into ant hills and termite nests. Their pointy snouts are handy to push into the hills and nests, and their tongues, which are eight to ten inches long, can actually chase the insects around in their homes.

Their saliva is very sticky, and the insects stick to the anteaters' tongues as they pull them from the hills and nests.

Roy Pinney / Photo Researchers

M. Austerman/ Animals Animals

3. **Fingerprint ant art** The children will enjoy making fingerprint ants and using a yarn tongue that can move from ant to ant! For each child, prepare a piece of paper with an anteater's tongue by cutting a five-to-six inch piece of red yarn and stapling or taping it to the side of the paper so a child can move it around freely on the paper. Each child can push his or her first finger onto an ink pad (a Crayola® pad that doesn't stain is convenient) and roll it on the paper to make an ink impression. Have them examine their special print. Explain that each finger has ridges and the fingerprint or pattern of ridges is unique to him or her. The children can use a magnifying glass to see the prints more clearly. Fingerprint "ants" can be pressed all over the sheet, and the "tongue" can be moved around to chase the ants.

More information about anteaters

> - *Anteaters live in Central and South America in swamps, forests, and savannahs.*
> - *Anteaters do not have teeth.*
> - *An anteater's tongue is eight to ten inches long.*
> - *There are three species of anteaters, and the giant anteater is the largest (about eight feet long from head to tail).*
> - *The giant anteater looks very awkward as it lumbers along because it walks on its knuckles in order to protect its long, sharp claws.*
> - *Anteaters sleep all night in trees and then hunt for insects during the day.*
> - *Anteaters have an extraordinary sense of smell and use their noses to search out different scents.*
> - *Mother anteaters carry their babies on their backs until the babies are a year old.*

Resources on anteaters

What Do Animals Eat?, by Ruth Belov Gross
Wildlife of the World, by Marshall Cavendish

Extensions

1. **Pinocchio** The Denver Zoo had an anteater named Pinocchio. Ask the children whether or not they have heard the story *Pinocchio.* Read the story to them or have a child who is familiar with the story summarize it for the rest of the children. Then talk with them about why the people at the Denver Zoo may have named their anteater Pinocchio. Do they think it is a good name for an anteater? Can they think of other storybook characters whose names would be good names for animals?

2. **How long is ten inches?** How long is a ten-inch tongue? Give children a long piece of yarn, a ruler, and blunt scissors. Have them measure a piece of yarn that is as long as an anteater's tongue. Using their "anteater's tongue" piece of yarn, challenge them to find objects in their environment that are the same length as the tongue.

3. **Song and game** Teach the children the song below. To add to its African sound, involve the children in making simple rhythm instruments that they can play along with the music. For example, rice, popcorn kernels, or pinto beans can be placed into metal adhesive-strip boxes or empty soda pop cans (the cans can be closed with masking tape). Make a drum can be made from an empty can such as a coffee can with the bottom removed and the plastic lid on top. Be sure to secure masking tape around the open end of the can to cover sharp edges. Then beat the drum on the accented beats in the song.

For a fun game of anteater and ant tag, have all but one child stand in a circle. The children forming the circle are ants. Have the remaining child stand in the center of the circle. This child is the anteater. On the word "Ants!" the anteater runs after the ants, and ants that are tagged become anteaters. Play continues until all ants have become anteaters.

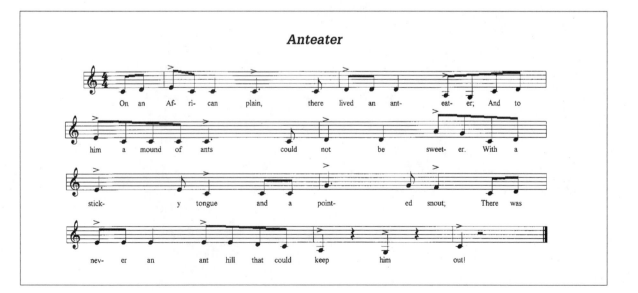

Anteater

On an Af- ri- can plain, there lived an ant- eat- er, And to

him a mound of ants could not be sweet- er. With a

stick- y tongue and a point- ed snout; There was

nev- er an ant hill that could keep him out!

Your tongue

 From *Elephants Are Wrinkly*, published by Good Year Books. Copyright © 1997 Susan Conklin Thompson.

Activities

1. **Tongues are tools** A tongue is an important tool. Provide the children with hand mirrors with which they can look at their tongues. Ask them to carefully observe their tongues as they stick them out. What do they see? What color are their tongues? Are they smooth, bumpy, or both? How are their tongues attached? Can they sketch their tongues?

What happens to your tongue when you talk? Have the children say a sentence while looking into the mirror. What happens to their tongues? Now have them say the same sentence while pressing down their tongues with a finger. What happens? Do their tongues play a role in their speech?

Explain to the children that a tongue is a set of muscles. It has one group of muscles that holds it to the back of the mouth and then

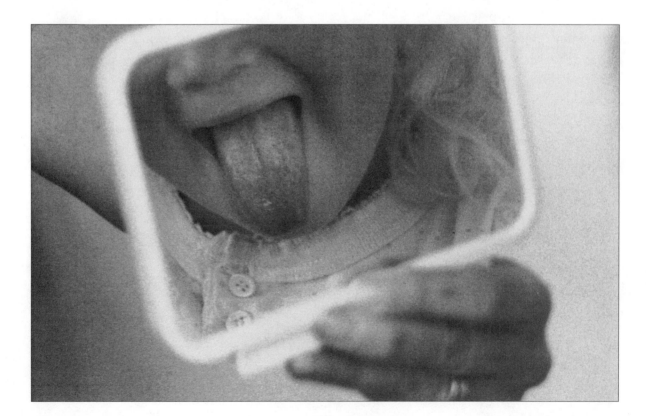

another group that controls the shape of the tongue and allows it to move around in the mouth. Can they move their tongues in and out? How about all around their mouths?

The book *In a Lick of a Flick of a Tongue*, by Linda Hirschmann, tells how different animals use their tongues. The book discusses how animals use their tongues to clean themselves, get food, and repair their homes. Read Linda Hirschmann's book to the children, or just talk with the children about how various animals use their tongues. Dogs use their tongues to pant. As the air passes from their tongues and into their throats, it cools them off. That is why dogs' tongues hang out of their mouths after a good run! Frogs are like anteaters in that they have sticky saliva on their tongues, and insects stick to their tongues like glue. Ask the children how many of them have ever drunk liquid through a straw. They will enjoy knowing that butterflies have a tongue like a straw through which they drink nectar. This tube is called a proboscis. Similarly an anteater collects ants in hills and termites in nests and rotten trees by chasing them with its ten-inch tongue.

2. ***What can you taste?*** The tongue can distinguish bitter, sweet, sour, and salty tastes through taste buds. The back of the tongue distinguishes bitter tastes, the middle of the tongue sour, the front sweet, and the sides salty. Have some mystery solutions for the children to taste. Unsweetened cocoa powder makes a bitter solution, sugar makes a sweet solution, lemon juice makes a sour solution, and salt makes a salty solution. Caution the children that they normally should never taste anything they are not familiar with because it could be poisonous. With a cotton swab, put a taste of one of the solutions in a child's mouth. Have him or her try to distinguish whether it is a sour, sweet, bitter, or salty taste. Then, try some of the other solutions. Be careful to use a new swab for each test and on each child. This will keep the test solutions pure and prevent the spreading of germs.

Sticky situations

From *Elephants Are Wrinkly*, published by Good Year Books. Copyright © 1997 Susan Conklin Thompson.

Activities

Tell the children that you are going to involve them in some very sticky situations. Then include them in making some sticky caramels, pulling an anteater's snout from a piece of taffy, and creating marshmallow ant hills.

1. **Making caramel** This can be done in a kitchen or on a hot plate. The children can help by measuring the ingredients and wrapping the candy when it is cool. Keep the children away from the burner and hot candy.

> *2 cups sugar*
> *2 cups heavy whipping cream*
> *3/4 cup light corn syrup*
> *1/2 cup margarine*

Put all the above ingredients in a saucepan. Cook over medium heat, stirring constantly, until the mixture boils. Heat until the mixture reaches 240°F on a candy thermometer or until the spoon is coated with a light, caramel mixture (may take up to 45 minutes). Pour into a greased 8-inch pan. After the candy cools, cut it into squares and wrap in waxed paper.

2. **Pulling an anteater's snout** Saltwater taffy can be purchased in candy and grocery stores and works well for this activity. Before you give the children the candy, tell them a shortened version of Rudyard Kipling's story "The Elephant's Child" or read the story to them. This story tells about an elephant that originally did not have a trunk. One day when the elephant was taking a drink out of the Nile River, a crocodile grabbed onto his nose and pulled and pulled until he pulled the elephant's nose into a long trunk. From that day forward the elephant has had a trunk.

Give each child a piece of taffy. The taffy works much better for pulling if it is soft. Have each child unwrap his or her candy. Explain to the children that they are going to pretend that they have an anteater in their hands. The anteater is going to go down to the Nile River the same way the elephant did. Have them pretend that their pieces of taffy (or anteaters) are walking down to the river. Lead them in pretending that their anteaters are getting a drink and then say, "Oh, No! A crocodile has grabbed the anteater's nose just like he did the elephant's!" Demonstrate for them how to pinch carefully a piece of the edge of the

taffy and how to pull carefully into the shape of a snout. Then each child can pretend that he or she is the crocodile, and, instead of letting go of the snout, he or she can say "snip-snap" and eat the anteater! Children can pop their taffy "anteaters" into their mouths for a fun treat.

3. **Marshmallow magic** Marshmallows are delightful because they are soft and puffy and fun but very sticky to eat. The marshmallows are made by creating a candy mixture that is filled with tiny air bubbles. This mixture is pushed through a tube onto a moving belt. The tube of marshmallows is dusted with cornstarch and then cut into marshmallow pillows. They are then dusted again with cornstarch before they are packaged. Some companies package marshmallows in plastic bags so they resemble pillows. They leave air in the bags to protect the marshmallows from being smashed when bags are piled on top of one another.

Have a bag of miniature marshmallows and one of large marshmallows available for the children to compare. Try to find packages that have been packaged with the air trapped inside the bags and look like pillows. Let the children feel the packages before they are opened. What do they feel like? Ask the children what it is about the packages that gives them that feeling. Lead them in thinking about the air that is trapped inside the bags. With the children, open the bags and then involve the children in the following activities, instructing them that these handled marshmallows are not to be eaten. (Hint: Keep a bag set aside for tasting afterward.)

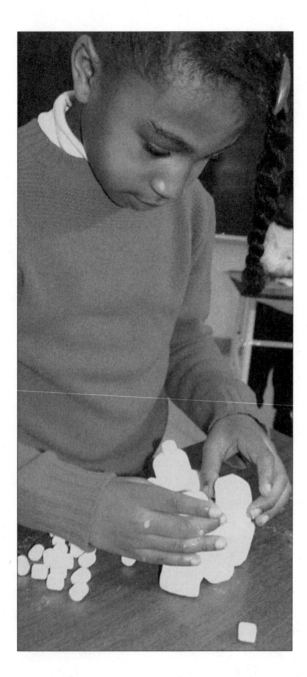

a. The children can compare the small and the large marshmallows. What do they notice? Ask them whether or not they have heard the word "miniature" before. Where, and in reference to what?

b. Challenge the children to think about how many miniature marshmallows they think would make up a large one. What can they do to estimate how many it would be? Some children may stack the small marshmallows to compare, others may squish the small ones into a ball, and some may try to weigh the small ones to match the weight of the larger. The large bag tells us that approximately ten miniature ones make up a large one. This will be interesting for the children to think about as they make their comparisons because they will point out that some are bigger than others.

c. Younger children will be challenged by counting ten or twenty or even one hundred marshmallows from the bag.

d. Ask the children whether or not they can make a tower from the miniature marshmallows. How tall of a tower can they make before it collapses? How about the big marshmallows? How tall before it collapses? Why do they think the bigger marshmallows can form a taller tower? Lead them in thinking about the concept of how the size of the base influences the height and design of a structure.

e. Be creative with the learning possibilities in math and science with the marshmallows. Wherever you are conceptually with the children, adapt an activity or think of a new one as you work with math and science concepts.

From *Elephants Are Wrinkly*, published by Good Year Books. Copyright © 1997 Susan Conklin Thompson.

Ant hill cookies

3 tablespoons margarine (plus extra margarine for molding cookies)
1 package (10 oz., about 40) large marshmallows or 4 cups miniature marshmallows
6 cups Rice Krispies® cereal
1 small package miniature chocolate chips
Vegetable cooking spray

Melt margarine in a large saucepan over low heat. Add marshmallows and stir until completely melted. Remove from heat. Add the Rice Krispies® cereal. Stir until well coated.

(Above recipe adapted from one on a box of Kellogg's ® Rice Krispies®.)

Instead of the common method of spreading the mixture in a pan, help the children grease their cleaned hands with margarine, and mold their own ant hill shapes with cereal mixture. Then they can wash their hands and carefully place miniature chocolate chips on the hills for ants. The "ants" can walk up and over the hill or be scattered around the top of the hill. When the ant hills cool and become firmer, they will be delicious treats for children, even though the children don't have sticky tongues or normally eat ants!

"Pet day

Activities

1. **Read a story** Read this short story to children and then involve them in the activities that follow.

Charlotte

Joe was excited about pet day at his school. Mrs. Barlett had told the children that on Tuesday they could bring their favorite pets to school. Joe was particularly excited because Mrs. Barlett had said that she was going to give a special prize to the child whose pet could perform the most interesting trick. Joe was sure that his pet, Charlotte, could win.

Joe left for school early on Tuesday, hiding his pet in a rough, brown gunnysack. He carried it carefully so Charlotte would not jostle around and get frightened. Joe also kept the bag open slightly so Charlotte could breathe. He walked quickly, looking down at the ground, until he reached the school grounds.

When Joe walked into the room, a big, shaggy dog jumped up onto him and he almost fell to the ground with Charlotte. Then Suzy said, "Rug, get down! Sorry Joe!" Rug was

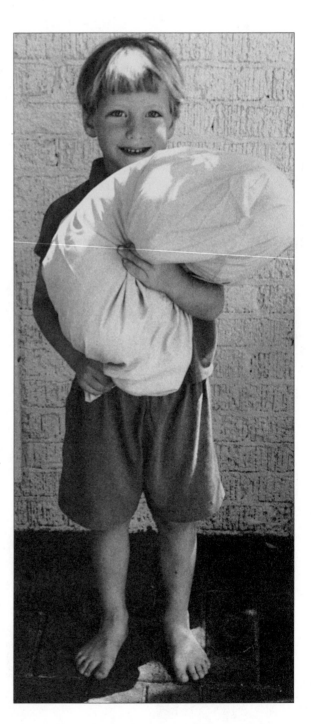

a great name, thought Joe. The dog jumped down as Suzy pulled on the leash. Joe looked around and saw Jeff with a parrot on his shoulder, Dan with a lizard in a cage, and Rosy with a large, white duck in her arms. Everyone else in the room seemed to have a dog. Joe thought all the little dogs looked the same, and they all seemed to be yipping the same way.

Mrs. Barlett, the first-grade teacher said, "All right, boys and girls. First of all, I would like everyone to introduce his or her pet. After you introduce your pet, show us any trick your pet can do. Jeff, why don't we start with you."

Jeff told the class that his parrot's name was Sam. Sam was cool, thought Joe. Sam told the class hello after Jeff said hello. The next pet was Suzy's Rug. Rug could pant really well. Then it was Sara's turn. Her pet was a mystery because she had it in a pillow sack. Everyone got quiet and waited to see what she would show. "This is my ant farm," called out Sara, as she took a large jar filled with dirt from the sack. "Oh, no!"

thought Joe. "An ant farm!" He grabbed tightly onto his bag and thought, "That could mean trouble." Sara was blabbing away about how she caught the ants, put them in the dirt, and fed them pieces of wet bread every night. Her trick was the great tunnels these ants could dig. When Sara was done telling about her very intelligent ants, she set the jar on the desk behind her.

Then some dogs caught some balls, one sat up and begged, and another little white dog shook his friend Lisa's hand. Then it was Joe's turn. Just as Joe reached inside his bag to pull out Charlotte, Suzy's dog Rug jumped up and knocked into the desk on which Sara's ant farm was resting. The jar crashed to the ground, spilling dirt and ants everywhere. Joe thought, "Oh, no, I can't get Charlotte out now!" Quickly, Joe went up to Mrs. Barlett and whispered something in her ear. She told him to take his pet and go into the hall. All the other children wondered why Joe was leaving. Mrs. Barlett got

a jar down from the science shelf and helped Sara scoop up the dirt and ants into another jar. Then she sent Sara into the hall to get Joe. Joe came quietly back into the room, carrying his bag. The children were very quiet as they watched Joe walk across the room to his spot in the circle. Then Mrs. Barlett said, "Joe has a very special and unusual pet inside his sack. Go ahead, Joe, and get her out and tell us all about her."

Joe reached inside the bag and pulled out the most unusual animal that his friends had ever seen. Charlotte was about the size of a cat. She was beige, had a long, tube-shaped nose; a long, dark brown, striped tail; and a dark brown patch on her back. She had long, sharp claws and small ears. "This is Charlotte," began Joe. "Charlotte is a baby anteater. She will grow up to be about eight feet long and two feet tall. My uncle is visit-ing me from Africa, and he brought Charlotte with him to add to the anteaters at the zoo."

Charlotte was scared and tried to get back into the bag. Joe had trouble holding on to her. "Charlotte is pretty scared right now, so I guess she won't be able to do her trick." Mrs. Barlett helped Joe get Charlotte back into the bag.

Joe looked at Sara and smiled. "Charlotte has this long, sticky tongue and is great at licking up ants, but today I was going to use a raisin!" Sara gasped slightly and clutched her ant farm into her arms. Mrs. Barlett smiled. "Hey, Mrs. Barlett," said Sam. "So that's why Joe went into the hall! When Sara spilled her ants, Charlotte could have had supper! I think Joe should get the prize for the trick his pet didn't do!"

Robert C. Hermes / Photo Researchers

2. ***I have an anteater's tongue*** After reading "Charlotte" to the children, talk with them about the story. Then tell them that they are going to pretend they have a tongue like Charlotte's, and they will get to pick up ants. Give each child a piece of double-sided sticky tape to place on his or her first finger. On the table, place small pieces of a dark colored yarn. As the children unroll their fingers and pick up a small piece of yarn, they can pretend that they are anteaters, the finger is their tongue, and the yarn pieces are really ants (don't let them actually eat the yarn).

Another fun tongue activity for children three years old and up is to give a party favor—one that unrolls when you blow into it—to a child. When he or she blows, have him or her think about why the favor uncurls. You will want to point out that the uncurling does not resemble the tongue of a frog or anteater, because their tongues extend rather than uncurl. That the tongue uncurls is a misconception many young children have from watching animated cartoons.

Sticky in nature

Activities

1. **Sap** There are many things in nature that are sticky. Ask the children to think about what they have touched or observed that is sticky. Among the responses, some children may talk about sap from trees and others may mention spider webs.

Pass around a piece of wood or a pinecone that has some sap on it. The children may lightly touch the sap and feel how sticky it is. Talk with them about how the sap can get into our clothing and is difficult to get out. The sap is really the "blood" of a tree.

2. **Maple syrup** Have some maple syrup available for the children to taste. Ask them whether or not they know how maple syrup is made. They may be very surprised to know that maple syrup is actually made from the sap of a maple tree. Show the children a picture of a maple tree in a book or, if there is one in your area, take them to the tree to observe it firsthand. Explain to them that a hole is drilled in the trunk of the tree and a spout is placed in the hole. The sap runs out into buckets and then is made into maple syrup by simply boiling it for a long time.

3. **Spider webs** Spider webs also are sticky but very useful to spiders. They eat the insects that fly or crawl into their webs. Spiders spin a web out of silk produced by their bodies. The webs are really a beautiful work of art and inspiring for young children to observe. Ask them to be careful about touching or tearing down a web because it is a spider's home. The designs of the spiders' webs can be recorded in an observation book through drawings, and the web drawings can be compared with one another.

Chapter 8   Textures together

❖ *21 texture activities*

I.

Visit the zoo

Integrated areas covered:

Science, Language Arts, Social Studies

Materials:
- plastic zoo animals (or toy animals from other materials such as wood)
- plastic fences (optional)

Getting started Different animals have various textures. Some are bumpy, some smooth, some hairy and shaggy, and others are wrinkly. Tell the children that today they are going to pretend that they are taking a trip to the zoo. Have a collection of plastic toy zoo animals available for them to examine and set up. Have a child hold up one of the animals, identify it, and describe its texture. Another child can hold up another animal and do the same. Help the child compare and contrast the first animal with the second. Is it larger? smoother? heavier? Is the plastic animal true to life? Many plastic zoo animals are not in proportion to one another. For example, the turtle may be larger than the gorilla. Talk with the children about what we mean when we talk about something being in proportion. Then divide the zoo animals into small groups (at least ten in each group if possible), and divide the children into groups so that each group of children will have some zoo animals with which to work.

From *Elephants Are Wrinkly*, published by Good Year Books. Copyright © 1997 Susan Conklin Thompson.

Activity

1. Examine each zoo animal.
2. Count the animals.
3. Decide on a way to group the animals.
4. Set the animals up as a zoo, with the grouping idea in mind.
5. Share why the zoo is set up like it is and how the animals are grouped.

Explore with children Are you grouping your animals by color, size, types, or different textures?

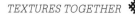

2. **Adopt a zoo animal**

Integrated areas covered:

Science, Math, Social Studies, and Language Arts

Materials

» play money

» pencils and paper

Getting started You and your children could be zoo parents! The Denver Zoo and the San Diego Zoo are looking for adoptive parents for their zoo animals. Explain to the children that various people and groups adopt zoo animals at different zoos around the country. They send money that goes to care for certain animals in the zoo. It costs a lot of money to feed the animals, hire the keepers, and take care of the animals' habitats. Talk with the children about which animal they would be interested in adopting and why. You can use play money to represent what it would cost to adopt a specific animal. For example, it might cost $50 a year to adopt a spider monkey, and $250 a year to adopt a llama.

Activity 1

1. Choose an animal to adopt.
2. Find out how much it costs or make up a cost.
3. Show the children how much money that is in play money.
4. Have them practice counting out the correct amount.
5. Choose another animal and amount and try again.

Activity 2

1. Gather additional information on being a zoo parent by writing or calling:

> *The Denver Zoological Foundation*
> *City Park*
> *Denver, CO 80205-4899*
> *Phone: (303) 331-4100*

> *or*

> *Adopt an Animal Program*
> *Zoological Society of San Diego*
> *P. O. Box 271*
> *San Diego, CA 92112*

2. If you live somewhere other than the Denver or San Diego areas, write to a zoo closer to home and see if it has an animal adoption program.

3. **A zoo in a box and a map of a zoo**

Integrated areas covered:

Science, Language Arts, and Social Studies

Materials

- ▸ boxes with one side cut away
- ▸ crayons and paints
- ▸ scissors
- ▸ glue
- ▸ stiff construction paper
- ▸ fabric, natural materials, and other optional supplies for habitats

Getting started Which animals live in a zoo? With the children, brainstorm various animals they know are in a zoo and write the names on the board or on a chart. Have pictures of animals available for children to classify into groups. Which would they group together? Why? For example, the lion, tiger, and panther are all cats and will be in the zoo in the cat house or feline area. Assign a group of animals to each small group of children. These may include bears, primates, cats, reptiles, hoofed animals, and birds.

With the children, discuss different animals' habitats. Encourage the children to think about what they have seen in different ani-

From *Elephants Are Wrinkly*, published by Good Year Books. Copyright © 1997 Susan Conklin Thompson.

mals' habitats or what they know each animal needs in its home to live. Some children will not have been to the zoo but can examine different animal habitats in books about zoo animals. One good book about habitats is *Zoos*, by Karen Jacobsen.

Demonstrate decorating a box to resemble an animal's habitat, and cut out animals, gluing them in the box. For example, a tiger's home would need places to walk, drink, and eat, and a tree would be nice.

Activity 1

1. Decorate a box to resemble a habitat, using construction paper, paints, crayons, fabrics, and natural materials.

2. Draw, cut out, and color animals for the habitat.

3. Glue the animals in the box. If the animal is to stand, a separate tab can be cut on the bottom of the animal and folded under and glued to the box.

4. As a group, place the boxes on a table or the floor, creating an entire zoo.

Explore with children What do you think a hippo would need to swim in, a monkey to climb on, and a fox to hide in? If you were the zookeeper, where would you feed the animals? What kind of plants or trees do you think the animals would need?

Materials

> ‣ paper and pencils
> ‣ crayons or markers

Getting started Look at a map (or the zoo map illustrated below) with the children. Explain that a map key tells what each symbol on the map represents, and the symbols on the map indicate where we can find things on a map. Different keys have various symbols indicating where things are.

Activity 2

1. On a piece of paper, draw a map of your own zoo.
2. Label where the types of animals are located.
3. Select symbols and create a key for the map.

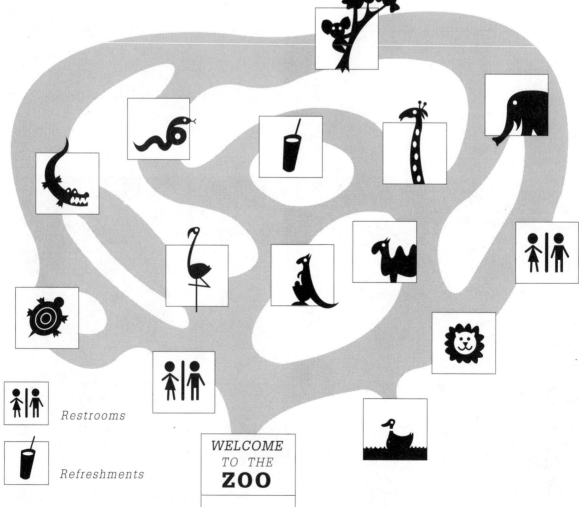

Restrooms

Refreshments

WELCOME
TO THE
ZOO

4. I know about many textures

Integrated areas covered:

Science, Language Arts, and Social Studies

Materials

- tag boards, blocks, or items with rough, smooth, bumpy, shaggy, and other textures. Suggested materials include sandpaper, sponge, velvet, corduroy, burlap, wire screen, waxed paper, and bark.
- glue

Getting started

Glue various materials that have different textures on 3-by-6-inch pieces of tag board or small wooden blocks (or use items, such as a scrub brush, that have distinct textures). Have the children rub their hands over one of the textures and describe the texture. Ask the children, "How does this feel?" They may respond, "This feels rough and scratchy." Then help the children make a connection to something in the world that is rough by asking what it reminds them of. They may answer, "This reminds me of rough cement on my bare feet."

Activity

1. Feel a textured card, block, or item.
2. Describe the texture.
3. Tell about something you know that feels the same or similar.

Explore with children Is there something in your home that feels like that? How about outside?

5. **Match a texture**

Integrated areas covered:

Science and Language Arts

Materials

- two cards each with rough, smooth, bumpy, shaggy, and other textures. Suggested materials include sandpaper, sponge, velvet and other fabrics, burlap, wire screen, waxed paper, and bark.
- 3˝ x 5˝ cards
- glue
- blindfolds

Getting started Make a set of texture cards by gluing various textures on 3˝ x 5˝ cards. Each texture should have two matching cards such as two cards each of sandpaper and velvet. Lay the different cards in random order on a table. Blindfold a child with a soft cloth and then let him or her feel the different cards and see whether or not he or she can find two that match.

Activity

1. Cover your eyes with a soft cloth.
2. Feel the different textures.
3. Find one or two pairs of textures that match and stack them together.
4. Describe/label the texture. ("This one is smooth.")

From *Elephants Are Wrinkly*, published by Good Year Books. Copyright © 1997 Susan Conklin Thompson.

Explore with children Can you find something that is smooth like silk? Something rough as when you move a bare foot across a rough sidewalk?

6. A texture hunt

Integrated areas covered:

Science, Social Studies, Language Arts, and Art

Materials

- crayons and other writing tools
- paper
- 3″ x 5″ cards
- glue (optional)

Getting started You can involve children in this game indoors or outdoors. Ahead of time, look around the environment to see which textures are available. Examples are bark on a tree may be rough, and sap may be sticky. On 3″ x 5″ cards write the names (or, for small children, glue pieces) of various textures children will be able to find. Have the children take paper and a crayon with them. When they discover something with the texture indicated on the card, they can record it different ways.

Throughout history, people have recorded observations and objects a variety of ways. Early cave drawings are a good record of events, as are journals. Hold up an item for the children to examine. Demonstrate ways to record the item through drawing, writing a description, and making a texture impression (lay a piece of paper on the object and rub the side of a crayon across the surface).

Activity

1. Pick several texture cards.

2. Locate objects or surfaces that have these textures.

3. Record the objects by drawing, describing in writing, or making a texture impression.

4. Share your findings with the group.

Explore with children Is one way to record better than another for different objects or surfaces? Can you take one object and try all three ways of recording the surface?

7. A textural collage

Integrated areas covered:

Science, Language Arts, and Art

Materials

- stiff paper or cardboard
- white glue
- materials with various textures such as corduroy and lace
- writing paper and pencils
- magazine pictures (optional)

Getting started Various textural materials can be glued onto a stiff piece of paper or cardboard to make a collage. To demonstrate, have several children each glue a piece of cotton, silk, sandpaper, or other materials onto an individual sheet of paper, or a large one if the group is to make a collage together. Talk with the children about what kinds of items would be good to collect (such as natural materials) or ask the children to bring from home things such as a sock, a foam packing peanut, potato sack, or objects that might fit with a theme, such as pieces of trash that have different textures.

Explore with children Which different textures are you using in your picture? How are you deciding where to put them on the paper?

Activity

1. Bring or find objects with various textures.

2. Glue the objects onto a stiff sheet of paper, making a collage.

3. Write a description about how the collage was made or a poem about the objects.

From *Elephants Are Wrinkly*, published by Good Year Books. Copyright © 1997 Susan Conklin Thompson.

8. Finger painting

Integrated areas covered:

Science, Social Studies, Language Arts, Music, and Art

Materials

- ▸ finger paints of several colors
- ▸ wet sponge
- ▸ paint smocks
- ▸ slick paper

Getting started Historians have evidence that the earliest known people painted with their hands and fingers, just as the people of today do. In 1929, an elementary teacher, Ruth Shaw, experimented with paints until she made a mixture that was safe and easy for children to use. Today, children every-where enjoy painting with their hands.

Explain that finger paints work best on paper that has a slick surface. Finger paint-ing can also be done on shelf paper, butcher paper, or even nonstick cookie sheets. Dampen a piece of paper that has a rough surface with water and have the children run their fingers across it. Then dampen a slick piece of finger painting paper with water and have the children feel the texture. Encourage them to compare and contrast what they feel. Talk with them about a kitchen floor that is wet from just having been mopped. Is it slick on their feet?

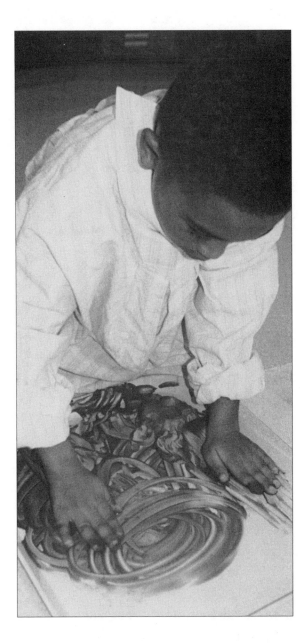

While the children watch, put a dab of finger paint on a sheet of slick paper that you have wet down by wiping with a sponge.

Demonstrate how to move a hand around in wide motions, make long, thin strokes with fingers or side of the hand, and use the thumbs for round prints and the fingernails for etching lines. Emphasize how interesting it is to experiment with the finger paint, and that if you do not create something you want, you can smooth out the paint and try again. A child may finger paint for a long time and never finish a finger painting. The process is thrilling in itself!

Activity

1. On damp paper, put a dab of one color of finger paint, or several small dabs of different colors.
2. Standing at a table, freely move your hands around in the paint.
3. Keep working with your paint and the picture until you get something you want.
4. If you want to make a print from your painting, lay another piece of paper over the top of your painting and pat it with your hand. Carefully lift it off the painting.
5. Talk about how the finger paint felt on your hands and about the process of moving your hands and fingers in the paint.

Explore with children What happens if we put on some music? Does slow music encourage different painting than livelier music? Are you using one hand or two? Do you think this should be called hand painting instead of finger painting?

Hints

1. Mixing two colors such as yellow and red to get orange is an interesting process in itself. How many different colors can the children make?
2. When the finger paintings are dry, they can be ironed on the back side so that they lie flat.
3. Objects other than fingers can be used to etch the painting such as a comb, a pinecone, or any item a child wants to try as he or she experiments with swirls and textures.

You and the children can make your own finger paint. Try the following recipe for finger paint and have fun experimenting!

Recipe for finger paint

1/3 cup cornstarch
3 tablespoons sugar
2 cups cold water
food coloring

Mix the cornstarch, sugar, and water together in a large pan, and cook it about five minutes until thickened (stir while it cooks). Remove the mixture from the heat and divide it into several cups or bowls. Add a different food coloring to each container and stir off and on while it cools. This finger paint works best when it is freshly made.

From *Elephants Are Wrinkly*, published by Good Year Books. Copyright © 1997 Susan Conklin Thompson.

9. Our feet feel

Integrated areas covered:

Science and Language Arts

Materials

> ▸ tub or bucket
> ▸ warm water
> ▸ sand
> ▸ towel
> ▸ sheet of paper
> ▸ crayons and pencils

Getting started   "What can you do with your feet?" Our feet help us balance when we walk, work well for turning the pedals on a bike, and help us swim. Our feet are very sensitive, and we can feel when the grass is soft, cool, or prickly, and the cement is wet, cold, or very hot. To stimulate children's thoughts as they feel a texture, have a large bucket or baby's bathtub filled with a few inches of warm water and sand.

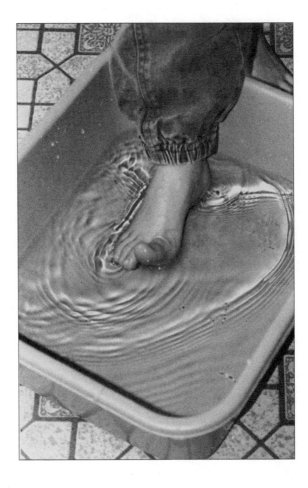

Activity .

1. Place a foot in the tub and feel the water and sand.
2. Scrunch your toes and swish your foot.
3. Describe how the water and sand feel.
4. Dry off your foot with a towel.

Explore with children   Have you felt this feeling of water and sand before? If so, when? What do you think gelatin would feel like? How about grapes?

Extension   Involve children in tracing around their feet and then writing something about their feet on the feet shapes. As a group, examine the foot tracings.

10. **What pet do you have?**

Integrated areas covered:

Science, Math, Social Studies, and Language Arts

Materials

- ‣ pictures of pets and/or animals from magazines
- ‣ bulletin board headings
- ‣ thumbtacks

Getting started Encourage the children to bring from home a picture of a pet they have. If they do not have a pet, have them bring a picture from a book or magazine of one they would like to have. Involve children in a simple pet graph on a bulletin board. Label different columns *Shaggy*, *Smooth*, *Rough*, *Wrinkly*, *Sticky*, and *Prickly*. You may wish to explore other ways to classify the pets, such as by natural habitats.

Activity

1. Bring a picture of a pet you have or one you would like to have.
2. Tell about the animal in the picture.
3. Describe the "texture" of the animal.
4. Pin your picture on a bulletin board under the texture heading.
5. With the group, read through all the animals in each heading.

Explore with children How many animals do we have in the shaggy column, in the smooth column, and so on? What are they? Where do these animals live in the wild? A nice beginning book of animal homes is *Animal Homes*, by Brian Wildsmith.

II.   **Every day a texture**

Integrated areas covered:

Science, Language Arts, and Art

Materials

> ‣ journals (and sketchbooks)

> ‣ pencils and/or crayons

Getting started For each child construct a small booklet in which to record different textural experiences during the day. Every day we feel many different textures. Talk with the children about different things they feel during the day that have various textures. For example, they may want to examine a loaf of French bread and describe in their journals that it is rough and bumpy on the outside but soft and fluffy on the inside. They may also want to make a sketch of the texture to go with the journal entry.

Activity

1.   Decorate the cover of your journal.
2.   Take the journal home with you over the weekend.
3.   Record different objects you touch during the day and their textures by drawing a picture and writing a few words about their textures.
4.   Share your journal with a friend.

Explore with children Where did you find the textures you recorded? How many different textures did you record?

133

12. **Making paper**

Integrated areas covered:

Science, Social Studies, Language Arts, and Art

Materials

- photo of a cocoon and a caterpillar
- paper to be recycled
- box to hold recyclable paper
- bucket of water
- blender
- screen with a frame
- tub

Getting started Show the children a picture of a cocoon and one of a caterpillar. Explain the life cycle of a butterfly. Tell the children that there are many other cycles around us. Help them think of other cycles such as a plant growing and reseeding itself, and their lives as they grow older.

Hold up a sheet of paper and ask the children whether or not they know the cycle of a piece of paper. Talk with them about how trees are cut down, made into paper at a factory, and then sold in stores. Explore the idea of cutting down the trees for the paper. Help the children think about how there is only a limited number of trees. We call trees a renewable resource because they replenish themselves naturally. However, they eventually will be gone if we cut them down faster than new trees can grow.

Ask the children, "What do we do with paper after we use it?" Talk with them about how the paper is burned, buried, or recycled. Encourage them to think of ways we can use less paper (for example, not using paper plates). Explain that we can recycle the paper so it can be used again. Many schools have paper recycling programs. To recycle paper and make new paper from the pulp, you can place a box in the room into which children can put used pieces of paper. After used paper has  accumulated in the box, lead the children through the following method of recycling and creating new paper. They can make many interesting textures on the sheets of paper that they make.

From *Elephants Are Wrinkly*, published by Good Year Books. Copyright © 1997 Susan Conklin Thompson.

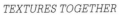

Activity You can involve the children in any steps they are developmentally ready for. As an example, many children will be able to participate in all the steps except using the blender.

1. Soak sheets of paper in a tub or bucket of warm water until they are thoroughly soaked. This will take several hours.

2. When the paper is thoroughly moistened, place a handful (about the size of an egg) into a blender 3/4 full of water.

3. Blend for about 20 seconds in water to make a fine pulp.

4. Lay a framed screen in the bottom of a dishwashing tub, bathtub, or other fairly large, flat container. (Hardware stores sell screened inserts for windows, which work well for the framed screen. You can also make one or have one made for you. The size can be chosen so that the screen fits easily into the tub.)

5. Place several batches of pulp onto the screen.

6. Pick up the screen with the paper pulp on it and, without tilting it, hold it horizontally above the tub while the water drains out.

7. Carefully, with your hands, pat the paper onto the screen, making textural impressions.

8. Set the screen in a sheltered place outdoors, tilting the screen so it will drain and the paper will dry more easily.

9. Let the paper dry for a day or two. Carefully peel it off the screen.

Explore with children Would you like to add flower petals, leaves, or something else into the pulp in the tub to give the paper some variety? Using your hands, which kinds of textural designs can you make on the wet paper? Do you think you could use other tools to make some textural variations?

Variation The children may pat the paper pulp with bark, an old shoe tread, or other objects for a more creative look. Or you can have the children press a board on top of the pulp on the screen to remove the water, and then they may lay the flat pulp over the object and leave it on until it dries.

An interesting book to share with children that takes them through the papermaking process in a factory is *Paper, Paper, Everywhere*, by Gail Gibbons.

13.

Shoes and you

Integrated areas covered:

Science, Social Studies, and Language Arts

Materials

› different types of shoes including a boot, dress shoe, and slipper

Getting started Show the children a shoe, such as a hiking boot that has a large tread. Then show them one with a smooth sole like a dress shoe. Which one slides more easily? The children can take a shoe and try to slide the sole across the floor. Does it slide easily? As they try each shoe, they can put it into a pile labeled "slides easily" or one labeled "does not slide easily." Why do some shoes slide more easily than others? Talk with them about how the tread creates friction on a surface and keeps you from slipping. Ask them to give examples of when it would be good to have tread on a shoe and also when a smooth-soled shoe would be easier to walk or run in. On the floor or on a table, lay additional shoes that have a variety of bottoms (for example, thongs, cleats, and ballet shoes).

Activity

1. Examine the bottoms of all the shoes.
2. Describe the sole of each one.
3. As a group or individually, arrange the shoes in groups ranging from the smoothest soles to the most rugged.
4. Remove your own shoe and see where it fits into the group.
5. Discuss the different shoes and what they might be used for.

Explore with children If you were on a beach, what kind of shoe do you think you might wear? Why? How does your shoe fit into this group?

14. # **Mystery rocks**

Integrated areas covered:

Science and Language Arts

Materials
- plastic bags of small rock particles
- rocks that correspond with particles
- paper labels for rocks displayed

Getting started Select several different rocks for the children to examine. Ahead of time, smash a piece of each rock into very small particles. Place the particles from each rock into separate plastic bags. Place the rocks and bags of particles on a table. Make a paper label for each rock (such as sandstone, shale, coal, and granite) and lay the labels on the table by the rocks (let the children match the labels and rocks later). Show the rocks to the children and explain a few things about each rock type.

Explore with children How do the various particles feel? Do they feel like the surface of a specific rock? How are you able to tell which rock goes with which card?

Activity
1. Carefully examine the particles in the different bags by looking at the textures, colors, shapes, weight, and powdery residue, and also at the rocks from which they came.
2. Guess which particles came from which rocks and place them together.
3. Examine how the different particles broke off the larger rock. For example, the sandstone breaks into grains, and sand grains can be seen in the large rock.

Extensions
1. Lay out the cards naming the rock types.
2. Examine the rocks' colors, textures, weights, and shapes.
3. Match a rock with a name card.
4. Talk about why you thought the rock belonged with the card.

From *Elephants Are Wrinkly,* published by Good Year Books. Copyright © 1997 Susan Conklin Thompson.

15. A textural feast

Integrated areas covered:

Science, Language Arts, Math, and Social Studies

Materials

- grater
- fine-mesh strainer
- a pot
- plastic gallon jug
- bowl
- spoon
- ingredients for butter listed below

Getting started making butter By using only a few simple ingredients, a person can make butter in a jug. Talk with the children about how the pioneers and maybe even their great-great-grandparents made their own butter in churns. Then involve the children in the following process to make their own butter.

Activity 1

Follow the recipe below to make butter.

Recipe for butter

*1/4 cup homogenized whole milk (use
    only whole)*
3 cups chilled heavy whipping cream
carrot and/or yellow food coloring

Grate a carrot and put the gratings in a pot with 1/4 cup milk. Simmer the mixture until it becomes a light carrot color. Yellow food coloring can also be added. The color will *fade as the butter is being made. Strain out the carrot pieces and set the colored milk aside.*

Pour the colored milk into a plastic one-gallon milk jug and add whipping cream. Fasten the lid tightly onto the jug. The children may take turns shaking the jug until the liquid becomes a heavy mush that they can't shake anymore because it is so thick (about 20 minutes). Help the children shake the mixture out into a bowl. To feel the mushy texture, the children can touch a small portion of the mixture set aside just for this purpose. Ask them to think about other substances they have touched that feel the same. Some children may think of mud and others of fudge that is cooling.

Pour the mixture through a fine-mesh wire strainer and discard the liquid. Dump the butter mush from the strainer into the bowl. Pour cool water into the bowl and mix it with the butter. Strain the butter again and throw away the water. Repeat this process until the water is clear and not a milky color.

Finally, press the butter against the side of the bowl with a spoon to get out the remaining water. The butter can be eaten right away or chilled and saved for later.

Materials

- French bread
- plastic knife
- newly made butter
- jam or jelly
- spoon

Getting started with the feast Cut a loaf of French bread into slices. Give a slice to each child. Lead the children in touching and feeling the rough outer layer of their bread and the soft, springy inside.

Activity 2

1. With a plastic knife, spread newly made butter onto the bread.
2. Touch the butter and describe the texture.
3. Add jam or jelly. Again touch and describe the texture.
4. Eat and enjoy the piece of bread.

Explore with children Can you describe the process we went through as we made the butter? Where does bread come from? How about jam or jelly?

Materials

- bowl
- spoon
- floured board
- loaf pan
- plastic knife

A feast for mice You and the children can make a very large loaf of bread, which will make a delicious treat for mice! After the loaf of bread is baked and cooled, involve the children in cutting windows and doors out of the loaf so that it will resemble a

"mouse house." Then find some friendly pet mice and put the loaf in their cage. What happens?

Activity 3

Recipe for mouse house bread loaf

1 1/2 quarts warm water
1 1/2 cakes fresh yeast
4 1/2 pounds wheat flour
1/2 cup sugar
2 tablespoons salt
1/2 cup plus 2 tablespoons shortening

Dissolve the yeast in the warm water. Stir in the flour gradually, until the dough is easy to handle. Add extra flour if needed.

Knead the dough on a floured board for about ten minutes. Put the dough in a warm place and let it rise. Punch down and let rise again. Put the dough in a greased 9x13x16- inch loaf pan. Bake the loaf 15 minutes at 425°F, and an additional hour at 325°. (A smaller loaf can be made by reducing the recipe by 1/4. Use a 9x5x3-inch loaf pan for a small loaf.)

(This recipe comes from a sign at the San Diego Zoo.)

Read *The Too-Great Bread Bake Book*, by Gail Gibbons, for a fun tale about a woman who bakes bread. It also includes a recipe for baking bread and illustrations of the process.

From *Elephants Are Wrinkly*, published by Good Year Books. Copyright © 1997 Susan Conklin Thompson.

16. The ABCs of textures

Integrated areas covered:

Science, Language Arts, and Art

Materials

» paper
» supplies for illustration
» ABC books to read

Getting started Share a collection of ABC books with the children. These may be checked out at your local public library. Talk with them about how some are based on themes such as animals, rhymes, or poems. Challenge the children, as a group or individually, to write an ABC book about different textures in the environment. Encourage them to be creative and even illustrate their books with different textures. Work through a few letters with them to help get them started. For example: *A* is for *acorns*, which are rough and smooth, *B* is for *bubble gum*, which is sticky when chewed.

Activity

1. Brainstorm textures through the alphabet.
2. Write text and create illustrations.
3. Share them with a friend, who may be a younger child.

Explore with children Does your book rhyme, is it descriptive, or both? How are you selecting a way or ways to illustrate your book? Are you going to paint, draw, or create a collage for each page?

17. **Eggs with contrasting textures**

Integrated areas covered:

Science, Language Arts, and Art

Materials

- photo of snake
- hard-boiled egg
- heavy paper or tag board cut in egg shapes
- materials with various textures, such as feathers, crinkled paper bags, yarn
- glue

Getting started Show the children a model or photograph of a snake or ask someone in your community to bring a pet snake to class. Ask them whether or not they have ever felt a snake. Ask them how it felt or how they think it would feel. Some children may be surprised to know that a snake feels very smooth and is dry so it almost feels slick! Help them understand that some things look different than they really feel.

Next let children hold a hard-boiled egg. How does it feel? It will also be very smooth and dry. Explain that for an interesting project they are going to be given an egg-shaped paper cutout, and they can make the egg any texture they want. Have a variety of fabrics and materials available to glue onto their eggs.

Activity

1. Select some materials to change the texture of the egg cutout.
2. Arrange them on the paper egg.
3. Glue on the materials.
4. Talk about how the different textural materials change the look of the egg.

Explore with children What is the opposite of *smooth*? What other textures do you know that are not smooth?

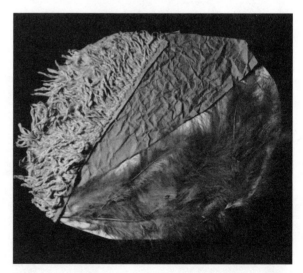

18. A self-portrait

Integrated areas covered:

Science, Social Studies, Language Arts, and Art

Materials

- self-portrait of a famous person
- variety of materials such as wood shavings, wallpaper, and pipe cleaners
- stiff paper or tag board
- pencils and/or crayons
- white glue
- writing paper

Getting started Explain that a self-portrait is a picture someone draws or paints of himself or herself. Show the children a self-portrait of someone famous such as painter Vincent Van Gogh. Then involve the children in making a different kind of self-portrait. For a fun twist to a self-portrait, involve the children in drawing themselves and then gluing on old braiding, curled wood shavings, net bags in which grapes are sold, or other unusual materials that will give their portrait some very interesting textures.

Activity

1. Look into a mirror and make an outline of your head.
2. Draw in details.
3. Glue on materials to make your portrait "colorful."
4. Share your artwork with a friend.
5. Write a poem or short piece about yourself to attach to your self-portrait.

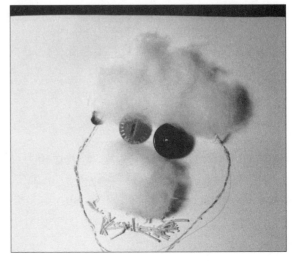

19. Sculpting people in sand

Integrated areas covered:

Science and Art

Materials

▸ sand

▸ sand table, sand box, or sandy beach

▸ spoons and other tools

▸ pieces of clothing

▸ bar of soap

▸ a stone

▸ piece of clay

Getting started Sculptures can be made from stone, soap, clay, or even sand! Different materials are sculpted in different ways. Let children feel a bar of soap, a stone, clay, and sand. How do the different materials feel? Talk with them about how we carve soap with a sharp tool, we use a chisel to knock small pieces out of stone, we pinch clay, and we pat sand.

Activity

1. In a sand box or at a sandy shore, sculpt a flat sculpture (small amounts of water will hold the sand together).

2. Add one or more pieces of clothing such as a tie and a cap.

Explore with children What can you add to the sand to mold it more easily? Which tools would be good for us to use with the sand?

 From *Elephants Are Wrinkly*, published by Good Year Books. Copyright © 1997 Susan Conklin Thompson.

20. Kallie Young, inventor!

Integrated areas covered:

Science, Language Arts, Social Studies, and Art

Materials

- ▸ chalk
- ▸ water
- ▸ resealable plastic bags
- ▸ paintbrushes

Getting started Read the following information about Kallie Young to the children.

Kallie Young is almost six years old, and she lives with her sister, mom, and dad in Cheyenne, Wyoming. Kallie is an inventor. She likes to experiment with the things around her. Chalk paint is her latest invention.

Kallie draws pictures and designs with chalk on her front porch and sidewalk. One day she was drawing and experimenting with chalk, and she discovered something new.

"I rubbed the chalk on the sidewalk until it got dusty. Then I tried to pick it up but it kind of faded, so I scooped it up and put it in a plastic bag. I found that if I added water to the bag of chalk dust and shook the bag, I could make colored water. Blue, purple, and pink are my favorite colors for bags of chalk water. I take the bags of colored water, and I use a paintbrush to paint with them on the sidewalk.

"I was not really surprised that this worked. I thought that if I added water the chalk dust would dissolve and turn into pink water, and it did.

"If the chalk and ground are wet, you can rub really hard with the chalk and it will rub off like dough. Then you can take the dough and roll it into little chalk balls to use later when you are drawing or making designs."

Activity
1. Make chalk drawings on a sidewalk.
2. Gather some chalk dust into a resealable bag, one for each color.
3. Add enough water to make the chalk liquefy.
4. Paint on the sidewalk with the colored water.

Explore with children Pretend you are an inventor. What would you invent?

From *Elephants Are Wrinkly*, published by Good Year Books. Copyright © 1997 Susan Conklin Thompson

21. **Papier-mâché animals**

Integrated areas covered:

Science, Social Studies, and Art

Materials

- ▸ papier-mâché
- ▸ cardboard
- ▸ masking tape
- ▸ paper towel or toilet paper rolls
- ▸ paper towels
- ▸ newspaper or scrap paper strips
- ▸ paint and paintbrushes

Getting started With the children, make the following papier-mâché recipe on page 148. Talk with them about how different animals have different textures, and that papier-mâché can be scrunched, folded, and manipulated in other ways to demonstrate textures. On a piece of cardboard, help the children to create the form of an animal, using paper towel or toilet paper rolls, tape, wadded and twisted paper towels, and scrap pieces of cardboard. Then help them drape the papier-mâché mixture over their animals, creating the desired textures.

Activity

1. Create an animal by taping together pieces of cardboard, paper towel rolls, and other materials.

2. Cover your animal with the papier-mâché mixture (take paper soaked in mixture and drape over animal form,

creating textures such as wrinkles for elephants, and bumps for crocodiles).

3. When your animal is dry, paint it any color you wish.

Explore with children Can you discover a way to make a texture that seems furry? How about smooth like the flamingo, or rough like the rhino?

Recipe for papier-mâché

3 cups water
1 1/2 cups flour

Mix flour and water and then cook mixture over low heat until mixture thickens to a paste. If too thick, add more water. Cool before using. Tear newspapers or other paper into strips and soak them in the papier-mâché paste.

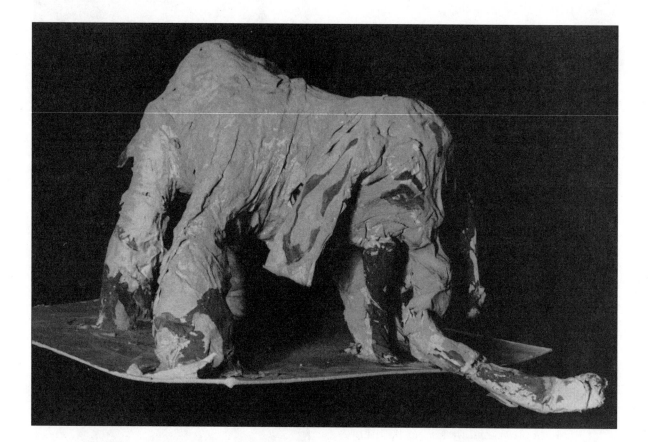

Professional resources

Andersen, Hans Christian. *The Emperor's New Clothes.* E. P. Dutton, 1991.

Anno, Mitsumasa. *Flea Market.* Philomel Books, 1984.

Arnold, Caroline. *Camel.* Morrow Junior Books, 1992.

Arnold, Caroline. *Flamingo.* Morrow Junior Books, 1991.

Baylor, Byrd. *We Walk in Sandy Places.* Charles Scribner's Sons, 1976.

Caudill, Rebecca. *A Pocketful of Cricket.* Holt, 1989.

Cavendish, Marshall. *Wildlife of the World.* Marshall Cavendish, Volumes #1 and #9, 1993.

Claudsley-Thompson, John. *Camels.* Raintree Children's Books, 1980.

Crowcroft, Peter. *Australian Marsupials.* McGraw-Hill Book Company, 1972.

Dragonwagon, Crescent. *The Itch Book.* Simon and Schuster, 1990.

Earle, Olive. *Camels and Llamas.* William Morrow and Company, 1961.

Gibbons, Gail. *Paper, Paper, Everywhere.* Harcourt Brace Jovanovich, 1984.

——. *The Seasons of Arnold's Apple Tree.* Harcourt Brace Jovanovich, 1983.

——. *The Too-Great Bread Bake Book.* Frederick Warne, 1980.

Green, Carl R., and William R. Sanford. *The Koala.* Crestwood House/Silver Burdett, 1987.

——. *The Porcupine.* Crestwood House/Silver Burdett, 1985.

Gross, Ruth Belov. *Alligators and Other Crocodilians.* Four Winds Press, 1976.

——. *What Do Animals Eat?* Four Winds Press, 1971.

Guarino, Deborah. *Is Your Mama a Llama?* Scholastic, 1989.

Hirschman, Linda. *In a Lick of a Flick of a Tongue.* Dodd, Mead, and Company, 1980.

Hoban, Tana. *Over, Under, and Through.* Simon and Schuster, 1987.

——. *Shapes, Shapes, Shapes.* Greenwillow Books, 1986.

Hunt, Patricia. *Koalas.* Dodd, Mead, and Company, 1980.

Irmengarde, Eberle. *Koalas Live Here.* Doubleday and Company, 1967.

Jacobson, Karen. *Zoos.* Childrens Press, 1982.

Johnston, Tony. *The Cowboy and the Black-Eyed Pea.* Putnam, 1992.

Keats, Ezra Jack. *Clementina's Cactus.* The Viking Press, 1982.

Kipling, Rudyard. *Just So Stories.* Viking Penguin, 1989.

Litchfield, Ada. *Words in Our Hands.* Albert Whitman, 1989.

Morrison, Susan Dudley. *The Alligator.* Crestwood House/Silver Burdett, 1984.

Robbins, Ken. *Tools.* Four Winds Press, 1983.

Sharmat, Marjorie Weinman. *Nate the Great.* Dell, 1977.

Stone, Lynn. *Crocodiles.* Rourke Corporation, 1990.

Thompson, Susan. *Hooray for Clay!* GoodYearBooks, 1989.

——. *Natural Materials.* GoodYearBooks, 1993.

Walker, Barbara. *The Little House Cookbook.* HarperCollins, 1989.

Wildsmith, Brian. *Animal Homes.* Oxford University Press, 1991.

Williams, Barbara. *Never Hit a Porcupine.* E. P. Dutton, 1977.

Wolff, Ashley. *A Year of Birds.* Puffin, 1988.

Wormer, Joe Van. *Elephants.* E. P. Dutton, 1976.

Yashima, Taro. *Umbrella.* Puffin, 1977.

Yoshida, Toshi. *Elephant Crossing.* Philomel Books, 1984.

Ziefert, Harriet. *A New Coat for Anna.* Alfred A. Knopf, 1988.

Zoll, Max Alfred. *A Flamingo Is Born.* G. P. Putnam's Sons, 1991.

Zolotow, Charlotte. *Hold My Hand.* Harper and Row, 1972.